THE CLAY SANSKRIT LIBRARY
FOUNDED BY JOHN & JENNIFER CLAY

EDITED BY

RICHARD GOMBRICH

WWW.CLAYSANSKRITLIBRARY.ORG
WWW.NYUPRESS.ORG

Artwork by Robert Beer.
Cover design by Isabelle Onians.
Layout & typesetting by Somadeva Vasudeva.
Printed and Bound in Great Britain by
TJ International, Cornwall on acid free paper

LOVE LYRICS

BY AMARU, BHARTṚHARI

TRANSLATED BY

GREG BAILEY

& BY BILHAṆA

EDITED AND TRANSLATED BY

RICHARD GOMBRICH

NEW YORK UNIVERSITY PRESS
JJC FOUNDATION
2005

First Edition 2005

The Clay Sanskrit Library is co-published by
New York University Press
and the JJC Foundation.

Further information about this volume
and the rest of the Clay Sanskrit Library
is available at the end of this book and
on the following websites:
www.claysanskritlibrary.org
www.nyupress.org

ISBN 978-0-8147-9938-3

Library of Congress Cataloging-in-Publication Data
Love lyrics / by Amaru, Bhartrihari, and Bilhana ;
edited and translated by Greg Bailey and Richard F. Gombrich.
– 1st ed. p. cm. –
(The Clay Sanskrit library) In English and Sanskrit;
includes translations and originals of Amaru's Amaruśataka,
Bhartṛhari's Śatakatraya, and Bilhaṇa's Caurapañcāśikā
Includes bibliographical references and index.
ISBN 978-0-8147-9938-3
1. Love poetry, Sanskrit–Translations into English.
I. Amaru. Amarusataka. English & Sanskrit.
II. Bhartṛhari. Śatakatraya. English & Sanskrit.
III. Bilhaṇa, 11th cent. Caurapañcāśikā. English & Sanskrit.
IV. Bailey, Greg, 1948–
V. Gombrich, Richard F. (Richard Francis), 1937–
VI. Series.
PK3701.L68 2005
891'.2100803543–dc22 2004026812

CONTENTS

A *sandhi* grid is printed on the inside of the back cover

Sanskrit alphabetical order

Vowels:	*a ā i ī u ū ṛ ṝ ḷ ḹ e ai o au ṃ ḥ*
Gutturals:	*k kh g gh ṅ*
Palatals:	*c ch j jh ñ*
Retroflex:	*ṭ ṭh ḍ ḍh ṇ*
Labials:	*p ph b bh m*
Semivowels:	*y r l v*
Spirants:	*ś ṣ s h*

GUIDE TO SANSKRIT PRONUNCIATION

a	b*u*t
ā, â	r*a*ther
i	s*i*t
ī, î	f*ee*
u	p*u*t
ū,û	b*oo*
ṛ	vocalic *r*, American p*ur*dy or English p*re*tty
ṝ	lengthened *ṛ*
ḷ	vocalic *l*, ab*le*
e, ê, ē	m*a*de, esp. in Welsh pronunciation
ai	b*i*te
o, ô, ō	r*o*pe, esp. Welsh pronunciation; Italian s*o*lo
au	s*ou*nd
ṃ	*anusvāra* nasalizes the preceding vowel
ḥ	*visarga*, a voiceless aspiration (resembling English *h*), or like Scottish lo*ch*, or an aspiration with a faint echoing of the preceding vowel so that *taiḥ* is pronounced *taih*^{i}
k	lu*ck*
kh	blo*ckh*ead
g	*g*o
gh	bi*gh*ead
ṅ	a*n*ger
c	*ch*ill
ch	mat*chh*ead
j	*j*og
jh	aspirated *j*, he*dgeh*og
ñ	ca*ny*on
ṭ	retroflex *t*, *t*ry (with the tip of tongue turned up to touch the hard palate)
ṭh	same as the preceding but aspirated
ḍ	retroflex *d* (with the tip of tongue turned up to touch the hard palate)
ḍh	same as the preceding but aspirated
ṇ	retroflex *n* (with the tip of tongue turned up to touch the hard palate)
t	French *t*out
th	ten*t h*ook

d	*d*inner	*r*	trilled, resembling the Italian pronunciation of *r*
dh	guil*dh*all	*l*	*l*inger
n	*n*ow	*v*	*w*ord
p	*p*ill	*ś*	*sh*ore
ph	u*ph*eaval	*ṣ*	retroflex *sh* (with the tip of the tongue turned up to touch the hard palate)
b	*b*efore	*s*	hi*ss*
bh	a*bh*orrent	*h*	*h*ood
m	*m*ind		
y	*y*es		

CSL PUNCTUATION OF ENGLISH

The acute accent on Sanskrit words when they occur outside of the Sanskrit text itself, marks stress, e.g. Ramáyana. It is not part of traditional Sanskrit orthography, transliteration or transcription, but we supply it here to guide readers in the pronunciation of these unfamiliar words. Since no Sanskrit word is accented on the last syllable it is not necessary to accent disyllables, e.g. Rama.

The second CSL innovation designed to assist the reader in the pronunciation of lengthy unfamiliar words is to insert an unobtrusive middle dot between semantic word breaks in compound names (provided the word break does not fall on a vowel resulting from the fusion of two vowels), e.g. Maha·bhárata, but Ramáyana (not Rama·áyana). Our dot echoes the punctuating middle dot (·) found in the oldest surviving forms of written Sanskrit, the Ashokan inscriptions of the third century BCE.

The deep layering of Sanskrit narrative has also dictated that we use quotation marks only to announce the beginning and end of every direct speech, and not at the beginning of every paragraph.

CSL PUNCTUATION OF SANSKRIT

The Sanskrit text is also punctuated, in accordance with the punctuation of the English translation. In mid-verse, the punctuation will not alter the *sandhi* or the scansion. Proper names are capitalized, as are the initial words of verses (or paragraphs in prose texts). Most Sanskrit metres have four "feet" *(pāda):* where possible we print the common *śloka* metre on two lines. The capitalization of verse beginnings makes it easy for the reader to recognize longer metres where it is necessary to print the four metrical feet over four or eight lines. In the Sanskrit text, we use French *Guillemets* (e.g. *«kva saṃcicīrṣuḥ?»*) instead of English quotation marks (e.g. "Where are you off to?") to avoid confusion with the apostrophes used for vowel elision in *sandhi*.

Sanskrit presents the learner with a challenge: *sandhi* ("euphonic combination"). *Sandhi* means that when two words are joined in connected speech or writing (which in Sanskrit reflects speech), the last letter (or even letters) of the first word often changes; compare the way we pronounce "the" in "the beginning" and "the end."

In Sanskrit the first letter of the second word may also change; and if both the last letter of the first word and the first letter of the second are vowels, they may fuse. This has a parallel in English: a nasal consonant is inserted between two vowels that would otherwise coalesce: "a pear" and "an apple." Sanskrit vowel fusion may produce ambiguity. The chart at the back of each book gives the full *sandhi* system.

Fortunately it is not necessary to know these changes in order to start reading Sanskrit. For that, what is important is to know the form of the second word without *sandhi* (pre-*sandhi*), so that it can be recognized or looked up in a dictionary. Therefore we are printing Sanskrit with a system of punctuation that will indicate, unambiguously, the original form of the second word, i.e., the form without *sandhi*. Such *sandhi* mostly concerns the fusion of two vowels.

In Sanskrit, vowels may be short or long and are written differently accordingly. We follow the general convention that a vowel with no mark above it is short. Other books mark a long vowel either with a bar called a macron (*ā*) or with a circumflex (*â*). Our system uses the macron, except that for initial vowels in *sandhi* we use a circumflex to indicate that originally the vowel was short, or the shorter of two possibilities (*e* rather than *ai*, *o* rather than *au*).

When we print initial *â*,	before *sandhi* that vowel was *a*
î or *ê*,	*i*
û or *ô*,	*u*
âi,	*e*

âu,	*o*
ā,	*ā* (i.e., the same)
ī,	*ī* (i.e., the same)
ū,	*ū* (i.e., the same)
ē,	*ī*
ō,	*ū*
āi,	*ai*
āu,	*au*

', before *sandhi* there was a vowel *a*

FURTHER HELP WITH VOWEL SANDHI

When a final short vowel (*a*, *i* or *u*) has merged into a following vowel, we print ' at the end of the word, and when a final long vowel (*ā*, *ī* or *ū*) has merged into a following vowel we print " at the end of the word. The vast majority of these cases will concern a final *a* or *ā*.

Examples:

What before *sandhi* was *atra asti* is represented as *atr' âsti*

atra āste	*atr' āste*
kanyā asti	*kany" âsti*
kanyā āste	*kany" āste*
atra iti	*atr' êti*
kanyā iti	*kan" êti*
kanyā īpsitā	*kany" ēpsitā*

Finally, three other points concerning the initial letter of the second word:

(1) A word that before *sandhi* begins with *ṛ* (vowel), after *sandhi* begins with *r* followed by a consonant: *yatha" rtu* represents pre-*sandhi* *yathā ṛtu*.

(2) When before *sandhi* the previous word ends in *t* and the following word begins with *ś*, after *sandhi* the last letter of the previous word is *c* and the following word begins with *ch*: *syāc chāstravit* represents pre-*sandhi* *syāt śāstravit*.

(3) Where a word begins with *h* and the previous word ends with a double consonant, this is our simplified spelling to show the pre-*sandhi*

form: *tad hasati* is commonly written as *tad dhasati*, but we write *tadd hasati* so that the original initial letter is obvious.

COMPOUNDS

We also punctuate the division of compounds (*samāsa*), simply by inserting a thin vertical line between words. There are words where the decision whether to regard them as compounds is arbitrary. Our principle has been to try to guide readers to the correct dictionary entries.

WORDPLAY

Classical Sanskrit literature can abound in puns *(śleṣa)*. Such paronomasia, or wordplay, is raised to a high art; rarely is it a *cliché*. Multiple meanings merge *(śliṣyanti)* into a single word or phrase. Most common are pairs of meanings, but as many as ten separate meanings are attested. To mark the parallel senses in the English, as well as the punning original in the Sanskrit, we use a *slanted* font (different from *italic*) and a triple colon *(⁝)* to separate the alternatives. E.g.

> Yuktaṃ Kādambarīṃ śrutvā kavayo maunam āśritāḥ
> *Bāṇa|dhvanāv* an|adhyāyo bhavat' îti smṛtir yataḥ.
>
> "It is right that poets should fall silent upon hearing the Kádambari, for the sacred law rules that recitation must be suspended when *the sound of an arrow ⁝ the poetry of Bana* is heard."
>
> Soméshvara·deva's "Moonlight of Glory" I.15

EXAMPLE

Where the Devanagari script reads:

कुम्भस्थली रक्षतु वो विकीर्णसिन्दूररेणुर्द्विरदाननस्य।
प्रशान्तये विघ्नतमश्छटानां निष्ठ्यूतबालातपपल्लवेव॥

Others would print:

kumbhasthalī rakṣatu vo vikīrṇasindūrareṇur dviradānanasya /
praśāntaye vighnatamaśchaṭānāṃ niṣṭhyūtabālātapapallaveva //

We print:

Kumbha|sthalī rakṣatu vo vikīrṇa|sindūra|reṇur dvirad'|ānanasya
praśāntaye vighna|tamaś|chaṭānāṃ niṣṭhyūta|bāl'|ātapa|pallav" êva.

And in English:

"May Ganésha's domed forehead protect you! Streaked with vermilion dust, it seems to be emitting the spreading rays of the rising sun to pacify the teeming darkness of obstructions."

Padma·gupta's "Nava·sáhasanka and the Serpent Princess" I.3

INTRODUCTION
BY GREG BAILEY

THIS BOOK presents collections of poems attributed to two figures—Bhartri·hari and Ámaru—famous in Indian intellectual history, but still largely unknown except for the literary legacy they have left behind. In using the names of Bhartri·hari and Ámaru we cannot be certain of designating specific individuals who were the authors of the poems included in the collections bearing their names. Biography in India—even of such celebrated figures as the Buddha and Shánkara—is hagiography, and in the case of both these poets hagiographical embellishments become important components in later interpretations (by commentators) of the poems. Two implications flow from this. First, we can only really speak about the Bhartri·hari and Ámaru collections as collections of poems that have been assembled into anthologies, usually by medieval commentators. Of the commentators' own sources we can never be certain. Second, we are required to disentangle and classify the later hagiographical elements in order to see whether they do provide a useful hermeneutical guide favoring a particular motivated reading of the poems.

Even to anchor the two poets in a chronological frame is difficult. The consensus of scholarly opinion is that Bhartri·hari is dated in the fourth century CE, Ámaru possibly in the middle of the seventh century.[1] But even if these dates could be confirmed with certainty they would not especially help us in understanding the way the poems should be read. In one respect, this kind of stanzaic poetry, where each poem stands independently of the others (as opposed to epic literature, where content often crosses verse boundaries), makes a virtue of ellipsis; it forces the reader to draw out the implication and suggestion in order to impose a meaning. But even so, the clearly defined themes that mark the "Hundreds" of both our poets distill aspects of culture to a set of specifics—sensuality and love, economic and social power, and rejection of society and culture—which they explore in a range of restricted variations, while omitting everything else. Even further restricting the possibilities of an Ámaru was the necessity to conform tightly to a set of conventions about poetic composition to which the sophisticated poet was increasingly adhering—while simultaneously exploiting the possibilities for variation within scholarly sanctioned strictures. The latter two points in particular affirm the elite status of this poetry and prevent its use as a source of history for all but a very narrow range of intellectuals and sophisticates. That such a group existed is, of course, a social fact of importance in its own right.

The placing together of Ámaru and Bhartri·hari in one volume is an opportunity for comparison, though contrast seems more appropriate in these two cases. While both poets worked within the narrow social and cultural sphere of Sanskrit poetry, and both may have had connection to kingship in some form or another, it is the differences between them that hit the eye. One would expect the task of comparison to begin with Bhartri·hari's *Passion (Śṛṅgara/śataka)* and Ámaru's *Hundred Verses (Amaru/śataka)*, as superficial similarities of imagery and theme readily appear. Yet the latter collection is as much about the social aspects of courting, betrayal, feminine indignance and masculine self-pity as it is about sensuality. Bhartri·hari's "Hundred" is primarily taken up with sensuality as a kind of cultural artifact and cultivated lifestyle, which in the ancient Indian context was either affirmed or utterly rejected in its capacity to function as a goal of human aspiration. The tension between affirmation and rejection occurs everywhere in Bhartri·hari's *Passion*, but leaves no trace at all in Ámaru. Because of this it is not possible to discern any perceptible line of development between our two poets, even if they are working with similar tools, though not necessarily under the strictures of identical poetic conventions.

Bhartri·hari's poems are much more physical and earthy in their presentation of women, focussing on the body,[2] in part to highlight disjunctions between image and substance, if not the constant deferral of any possibility of finding substance. Explicit criticism of *śṛṅgāra* (love as conceptualised by Indian literary theory) is a constant theme of "Passion," the *Śṛṅgāra/śataka*, the criticism often being so strident that the impulse for the composition of these poems can justifiably be seen as coming from a renunciatory perspective. This would mean that *Passion* is really a text coming from the "disenchantment" *(vairāgya)* postion, even though Bhartri·hari does also claim authorship of *Disenchantment*, the *Vairāgya/śataka*. In spite of the important late commentary on Ámaru's *Hundred Verses* by Ravi·chandra, which does give a Vedántic reading of the text[3], this is a reading that has to be elicited rather than accepted at face value as the principal ideological key to the poetry. A reading of Bhartri·hari's *Passion* from the perspective of dispassion is certainly not forced, and means the poet is undermining the ideological basis of his poetry as he is composing it.

Bhartri·hari is idiosyncratic within the tradition of Sanskrit poetry, a quality that has endeared him to Western readers. SIEGFRIED LIENHARD's judgment of the manifestation of this idiosyncrasy is apposite:[4]

> *Bhartri·hari's personality appears much more clearly in his work than is the case with the majority of classical Indian poets. It is characteristic of Bhartri·hari's lyrical poetry, particularly love poems, that they do not generally contain the usual lyrical scenes . . . The poet's pronounced intellectual leanings are unmistakable.*

By the time Ámaru was composing it may not have been possible to be as iconoclastic as Bhartri·hari. Thus Bhartri·hari's three hundreds and the tradition to which this has given rise are our principal context for understanding his own poetry, however much later commentators have tried to place them within the straitjacket of Indian æsthetic theory.

Ámaru is stylistically different from Bhartri·hari. He is more elliptical and makes much greater use of temporal disjunctions by the frequent employment of the locative absolute and gerunds. And, as SHELDON POLLOCK has shown, he demonstrates a development in the use of meter, utilizing a technique of controlled disjunction between syntactical and metrical units, in a way not evident in Bhartri·hari's poetry.[5] Now that we have machine-readable versions of the texts, POLLOCK's line of research can and should be taken further. A thorough stylistic analysis that begins from word order, syntax, meter, adherence and deviation from poetic conventions, and concentration of vocabulary, will show greater differences between the poetry of Bhartri·hari and

Ámaru than the differences in content and meaning superficially suggest.

THE TRANSLATIONS

While it is no longer helpful to appeal to the dictum that poetry can never be translated, it is incumbent upon the translator to explain something of the guidelines he has used. This is especially so when the poems presented have been translated before. In addition, the policy of the CLAY SANSKRIT LIBRARY is that translations should be as close as possible to the Sanskrit text, so that the reader can move easily from one to the other if desired. This is, of course, the aim of all bilingual editions, but as often as not, it is an aim observed in the breach.

To my knowledge, the poems of the Ámaru collection have received far less attention from translators than the Bhartri·hari collection have. This is so in spite of their fame, beauty and elegance, and their accessibility through a series of good Sanskrit commentaries. At one time or another all of the poems have been translated into the predominant European languages, and a few of them have been rendered brilliantly by JOHN BROUGH[6] and DANIEL INGALLS[7] in their well-known collections of Sanskrit poems.

Of the Ámaru collection there exists an excellent Italian translation[8] and a good French translation;[9] and many poems from the collection have been translated into German in OTTO VON BÖHTLINGK's *Indische Sprüche*.[10] The first two can accurately be described as translations into free verse and make no attempt to follow the meter, even if this just means mirroring distinct metrical feet into equivalent syntactic units where this is possible (as successfully achieved by Ingalls and more suggestively by BERNDT KÖLVER).

BÖHTLINGK offers prose paraphrases for each verse, as does the quite useful English paraphrase included in C. R. DEVADHAR's edition, which presents the text (with variants) as it occurs in Vema·bhu·pala's commentary entitled *Śṛṅgāra|dīpikā*.[11] This is the edition used in the Italian and French translations cited. DEVADHAR's paraphrase attempts to explain the full meaning of the poem, sometimes incorporating bits of the commentary, and does not claim to be a rendering of poetry by poetry, so it should not be judged on this basis.

The translation I offer is based on the edition of SRI PRADYUMNA PANDEYA and includes the important commentary of Árjuna·varma·deva entitled *Rasika|saṃjīvinī*.[12] This very edition is itself based on the more famous and older edition produced by the Nirnaya Sagar Press and reproduces what scholars call the Western recension of the poems.[13] It contains some poems not included in DEVADHAR's edition, though DANIELA ROSSELLA has translated them as an addition in her translation.[14] I have rendered them into free verse only in the sense of respecting brevity—sometimes to the point of ellipsis—of expression and the form of poetry. With almost minimal exception, each poem is a self-contained unit whose independence is recognized by the fact that many poems in the Ámaru collection so easily found their way into later collections. Ease of comprehension, I hope, has not been sacrificed, though the reader should bear in mind that the restricted number of connoisseurs of this poetry contemporary to Ámaru—the putative composer—would have possessed an education almost at the level of the poet himself. More substantial contextualization of the complex intertextuality operating in these poems would have been unnecessary for them. To later generations in South Asia and contemporary readers this condition does not apply, hence the appearance of several substantial analytical commentaries. DEVADHAR's and ROSELLA's notes go some way toward bridging the gap between poetic brevity and prose comprehension, and allude to some of the intertextual references in the poems.

Translation of Bhartri·hari's "Three Hundreds" *(Śataka/trayam)* is a different story. After the *Bhágavad·gita* it is probably the most translated of Sanskrit texts, and this should give us some insight into its reception history in the West. Knowledge of the text has not improved greatly since D. D. KOSAMBI's foundational synoptic edition of 1948.[15] Nor, sadly, has criticism of Bhartri·hari's poetry and thought—despite its uniqueness in Indian intellectual history during and after the Gupta period—increased in depth.

Typical of translators up until the mid-nineteen-sixties was the choice of three hundred poems of the Bhartri·hari collection and their translation as a whole, or the translation of specific hundreds, usually *Passion* or (especially in India) *Dispassion.* Since KOSAMBI's edition, the two most important translations (I exclude SEREBRYAKOV's Russian translation here, as it is inaccessible to most people outside of Russia) have followed that edition and have translated only the two hundred poems KOSAMBI considered as most likely to be by somebody called Bhartri·hari, in that they occur in manuscripts belonging to all the major recensional traditions. Barbara Stoler Miller's[16] translation is probably the one best known to English readers and reads very effectively as free verse. It does not mirror the form of the Sanskrit verses, most of which are restricted to four distinct lines, but Ingalls and Pollock are the only translators I know who have attempted to respect this poetic form. Where Stoler Miller's translations succeed is in their capturing of Bhartri·hari's skepticism and of his refusal to privilege any of the most powerful cultural positions of his day. Where they are at their weakest is in the very loose relationship her rendering bears to the Sanskrit original. Poetic flourish sometimes results in the sacrifice of sufficient mirroring of vocabulary, word order and the correlation of meter and syntactic structure.

The other important translation to have followed Kosambi's synoptic edition is that into Italian done by Alex Passi in 1989.[17] Although rendered into free verse—in a much more subdued manner than Stoler Miller's renderings—this translation is quite transparent in relation to the Sanskrit text and it is possible to jump from one to the other with relative ease. It does not, however, contain the translated text. I have found it to be quite valuable in completing my own translation.

Unlike Passi or Stoler Miller, I have returned to the older practice and have translated three hundred poems taken from the collection assembled and commented upon by the learned Maharashtrian commentator Rama·chandra·budhéndra.[18] As well as including three hundred poems, poems that overlap substantially, though not exclusively, with the poems commented upon by the two other important commentators—Ramárshi and Dhana·sára·gani—the individual poems within the hundreds are grouped into themes, which become quite apparent on reading the poems. Whether this is what the "original" poet Bhartri·hari intended cannot be known, and such a division is not reflected in KOSAMBI's great synoptic edition.

My own translation betrays is more literal than STOLER MILLER's, with which it is likely to be compared, even though Rama·chandra·budhéndra's text differs in many small ways from KOSAMBI's, on which her translation is based. Above all I have attempted to honor the brief that the translation should be as transparent as possible in relation to the source text. In moving toward such transparency I have tried to be faithful to the word order which seems to mirror the breaks of each line of verse by the caesura. This has been easier to achieve where there occurs only one caesura in each foot, especially in the case of the common *śārdūla/vikrīḍita* meter, much more difficult where there are two caesurae, such as in *srag/dharā* verses. Sometimes this may have led to some slightly stilted or seemingly overcontrived translations, but I believe the effort is justified if it successfully communicates the sense in which Bhartri·hari allows syntactic units to mirror metrical units. I have not been able to achieve the same level of mirroring with Ámaru, because of more complex and deliberate disjunction between metrical unit and syntactic form.

Notes

1 S. Lienhard, *A History of Classical Poetry. Sanskrit-Pāli-Prakrit* (Otto Harrassowitz, Wiesbaden, 1984), pp. 90–92.

2 See Greg Bailey, *Bhartṛhari's Critique of Culture* (Melbourne, La Trobe University, Asian Studies Papers—Research Series, 2, 1994); "Bhartṛhari's manipulation of the feminine," *Indo-Iranian Journal*, 39, (1996), pp. 201–221.

3 Yigal Bronner, "Double-Bodied Poet, Double-Bodied Poem: Ravicandra's Commentary on the Amaruśatakam and the Rules of Sanskrit Literary Interpretation," *Journal of Indian Philosophy* (1998), pp. 233–261.

4 Lienhard, *op.cit.* p. 90. Perhaps only poems 21 and 66 of the *Śṛṅgāra/śataka*, both developing the theme of love-in-separation, are comparable to what is so common in the *Amaru/śataka*.

5 S. Pollock, *Aspects of Versification in Sanskrit Lyric Poetry* (American Oriental Society, New Haven, 1977). A recent article by B. Kölver suggests a new line of investigating meter. This is also of great interest here in demonstrating how some of the poems in the Sikhariṇī meter in Ámaru contain poems in poems where fragments of distinct poems can be discerned in the words preceding the caesura. See B. Kölver, "Poems Within Poems: Śikhariṇī in Amaru," in M. Juntunen, W. L. Smith and C. Suneson, eds., *Sauhṛdyamaṅgalam. Studies in Honour of Siegfried Lienhard on His 70th Birthday* (The Association of Oriental Studies, Stockholm, 1995), pp. 189–205.

6 J. Brough, *Poems from the Sanskrit* (Penguin, Harmondsworth, 1968).

7 D. H. H. Ingalls, *Sanskrit Poetry, from Vidyakara's Treasury* (Belknap Press of Harvard University Press, Cambridge [Mass.], 1968).

8 D. S. ROSSELLA, *Amaruka. Centuria d'Amore* (Marsilio Editori, Venice, 1989).

9 A. REBIÈRE, *La centurie (Amaruśataka) Poèmes amoureux de l'Inde ancienne* (Gallimard, Paris, 1993).

10 BÖHTLINGK, OTTO VON, *Indische Sprüche: Sanskrit und Deutsch* (Otto Zeller Verlag, Osnabruck, 1966; reprint of the 2nd ed, St. Petersburg, 1870–73).

11 C. R. DEVADHAR, *Amaruśatakam. With Śṛṅgāradīpikā of Vemabhūpāla. A Centum of Ancient Love Lyrics of Amaruka* (Oriental Book Agency, Poona, 1959).

12 *Amaruśatakam of Śri Amaruka with the Rasikasaṃjīvinī Sanskrit Commentary by Arjunavarmadeva* and edited with the "Prakasa" Hindi commentary by ŚRI PRADYUMNA PANDEYA; introd. by ŚRI NARAYANA MIŚRA (Varanasi: Chowkhamba Sanskrit Series Office, 1966).

13 N. R. ACHARYA, ed., Amaruśatakam of Amaruka with the *Rasikasaṃjīvinī Sanskrit commentary by Arjunavarmadeva* (Nirnaya Sagar Press, Bombay, 1889, 1954).

14 See ROSELLA, *op.cit.*, pp. 77–82.

15 D. D. KOSAMBI, ed., *Śatakatrayādi-subhāṣitasaṃgraha: The Epigrams Attributed to Bhartṛhari* (Bombay, 1948).

16 B. STOLER MILLER, *Bhartṛhari: Poems* (Columbia University Press, New York-London, 1967).

17 A. PASSI, *Bhartṛhari. Sulla saggessa mondana, sull'amore e sulla rinuncia* (Milan, 1989).

18 D. D. KOSAMBI, ed., *Subhāṣitatriśatī* (Bombay, 1957).

BHARTRI·HARI: POLITICS

DIK|KĀL'|ĀDY|anavacchinn'|
ânanta|cin|mātra|mūrtaye
sv'|ânubhūty|eka|mānāya
namaḥ śāntāya tejase.

Boddhāro matsara|grastāḥ,
prabhavaḥ smaya|dūṣitāḥ,
abodh'|ôpahatāś c' ânye,
jīrṇam aṅge subhāṣitam.

Ajñaḥ sukham ārādhyaḥ,
sukhataram ārādhyate viśeṣajñaḥ,
jñāna|lava|durvidagdhaṃ
Brahm" âpi naraṃ na rañjayati.

Prasahya maṇim uddharen
makara|vaktra|daṃṣṭr'|ântarāt,
samudram api saṃtaret
pracalad|ūrmi|māl"|ākulam,
bhujaṅgam api kopitaṃ
śirasi puṣpavad dhārayen,
na tu pratiniviṣṭa|mūrkha|
jana|cittam ārādhayet.

5 Labheta sikatāsu tailam api yatnataḥ pīḍayan,
pibec ca mṛga|tṛṣṇikāsu salilaṃ pipās'|ârditaḥ,
kadācid api paryaṭañ śaśa|viṣāṇam āsādayen,
na tu pratiniviṣṭa|mūrkha|jana|cittam ārādhayet.

UNDIVIDED BY SPACE, time or qualities,
Whose form is nothing but endless consciousness,
Measurable only by his own awareness,
Tranquil and splendid. To him obeisance!

Consumed by envy are the learned,
Corrupted by arrogance are the powerful,
Destroyed by ignorance are the others,
Eloquence withers with the body.

An ignorant man is easily placated,
Still more easily placated is a specialist.
The man inflamed by a morsel of knowledge
Not even Brahma can please.

He may forcibly extract a jewel
From between a sea monster's fangs,
Even cross the ocean
Convulsed by garlands of pulsating waves,
Even a furious snake
He may wear on his head as a flower.
But the mind of an obstinate fool
He will not please.

He might even find oil in sand 5
By crushing it strenuously.
He might also drink water from a mirage
When desperately thirsty.
Sometimes, when wandering around,
He might even come upon a hare's horn.*
But the mind of an obstinate fool
He will not please.

Vyālaṃ bāla|mṛṇāla|tantubhir asau
roddhuṃ samujjṛmbhate,
bhettuṃ vajra|maṇiṃ śirīṣa|kusuma|
prāntena sannahyati,
mādhuryaṃ madhu|bindunā racayituṃ
kṣār'|âmbudher īhate,
mūrkhān yaḥ pratinetum icchati balāt
sūktaiḥ sudhā|syandibhiḥ.

Sv'|āyattam ekānta|hitaṃ Vidhātrā
vinirmitaṃ chādanam ajñatāyāḥ
viśeṣataḥ sarvavidāṃ samāje
vibhūṣaṇaṃ maunam apaṇḍitānām.

Yadā kiṃ|cij|jño 'haṃ
gaja iva mad'|ândhaḥ samabhavaṃ
tadā «sarvajño 'sm'
îty» abhavad avaliptaṃ mama manaḥ;
yadā kiṃ cit kiṃ cid
budha|jana|sakāśād avagataṃ
tadā «mūrkho 'sm' îti»
jvara iva mado me vyapagataḥ.

Kṛmi|kula|citaṃ lālā|klinnaṃ
vigandhi jugupsitaṃ
nirupama|rasa|prītyā khādan
khar'|âsthi nirāmiṣam
Sura|patim api śvā pārśva|sthaṃ
vilokya, na śaṅkate,
na hi gaṇayati kṣudro jantuḥ
parigraha|phalgutām.

A wild elephant, with a tender lotus thread
He attempts to restrain.
A diamond, with the edge of the silk flower
He equips himself to split.
The saline ocean, with a drop of honey
He desires to make sweet.
So is he who seeks ardently to guide fools
With wise sayings dripping with ambrosia.

Used at one's will and always beneficial, the Arranger*
Created it as a veil for ignorance.
Especially in an assembly of learned men
Silence is an adornment for the fool.

When I knew a little,
Like an elephant blinded by rut I became.
"I know everything,"
So my mind became stained.
When slightly more
From being near the wise I learnt
"I am a fool,"
So my arrogance like fever retreated.

Crawling with worms, slimy with spit,
Stinking, disgusting,
Delighting still in its superb flavor, a dog eats
The fleshless bone of a donkey.
Even if standing beside him the Lord of the gods
He sees, no shame he feels.
A wretch takes no account
Of how pathetic his possession is.

Śiraḥ Śārvaṃ svargāt
Paśupati|śirastaḥ kṣiti|dharaṃ
mahī|dhrād uttuṅgād
avanim avaneś c' âpi jaladhim
atho Gaṅgā s" êyaṃ
padam upagatā stokam atha vā
viveka|bhraṣṭānāṃ
bhavati vinipātaḥ śata|mukhaḥ.

Śāstr'|ôpaskṛta|śabda|sundara|giraḥ
śiṣya|pradey'|āgamāḥ
vikhyātāḥ kavayo vasanti viṣaye
yasya prabhor nirdhanāḥ,
taj jāḍyaṃ vasudh"|âdhipasya sudhiyas
tv arthaṃ vin" âp' īśvarāḥ,
kutsyāḥ syuḥ kuparīkṣakair na maṇayo
yair arghataḥ pātitāḥ.

Hartur yāti na gocaraṃ, kim api śaṃ
puṣṇāti yat sarvadā"py
arthibhyaḥ pratipādyamānam aniśaṃ
prāpnoti vṛddhiṃ parām,
kalp'|ânteṣv api na prayāti nidhanaṃ
vidy"|ākhyam antardhanaṃ
yeṣāṃ, tān prati mānam ujjhata, nṛpāḥ!
kas taiḥ saha spardhate?

From heaven to Sharva's head, 10
From Pashu·pati's head to Himálaya mountain,
From that lofty mountain,
To the Earth, and from Earth to the ocean.
So this same Ganges
has reached a reduced state.
For people whose discrimination is lost
There are one hundred possibilities of plummeting.

With voices beautified by refined words of sacred learning,
With teachings fit for transmission to pupils,
If famous poets live under
A king, yet are poverty-stricken,
Stupid is the king, but the wise,
Even without wealth are lords:
Reviled, may jewels be by inept judges,
But still they are not truly devalued.

Not accessible to a thief, yet invariably
Fostering a little happiness,
When bestowed on those desiring it,
Always attaining the highest increase,
It is not destroyed even at the end of a cosmic period.
Called knowledge is this inner wealth.
Kings, let go your haughtiness toward those who have it.
Who can compete with them?

Adhigata|param'|ârthān paṇḍitān m" âvamaṃsthāḥ
tṛṇam iva laghu lakṣmīr n' âiva tān saṃruṇaddhi,
abhinava|mada|rekhā|śyāma|gaṇḍa|sthalānāṃ
na bhavati bisa|tantur vāraṇaṃ vāraṇānām.

Ambhojinī|vana|vihāra|vilāsam eva
haṃsasya hanti nitarāṃ kupito Vidhātā,
na tv asya dugdha|jala|bheda|vidhau prasiddhāṃ
vaidagdhya|kīrtim apahartum asau samarthaḥ.

15 Keyūrāṇi na bhūṣayanti puruṣaṃ,
    hārā na candr'|ôjjvalāḥ,
na snānaṃ, na vilepanaṃ, na kusumaṃ,
    n' âlaṃkṛtā mūrdhajāḥ,
vāṇy ekā samalaṃkaroti puruṣaṃ
    yā saṃskṛtā dhāryate.
kṣīyante 'khila|bhūṣaṇāni satataṃ,
    vāg|bhūṣanaṃ bhūṣaṇam.

Vidyā nāma narasya rūpam adhikaṃ,
    pracchanna|guptaṃ dhanaṃ,
vidyā bhoga|karī, yaśaḥ|sukha|karī,
    vidyā gurūṇāṃ guruḥ,
vidyā bandhu|jano videśa|gamane,
    vidyā parā devatā,
vidyā rājasu pūjyate, nahi dhanaṃ.
    vidyā|vihīnaḥ paśuḥ.

Men who have reached the highest truths—
The *pandits*—despise them not.
Wealth is about as substantial as grass,
Them it certainly will not obstruct.
For elephants,
Lines of fresh rut
Blackening their cheeks,
A piece of lotus fiber is not an impediment.

Only the goose's dazzling play in lotus groves
Can the enraged Arranger utterly destroy.
But its famous skill in separating milk from water,
He has not the capacity to remove.

Armlets do not embellish a man,
Nor necklaces bright as the moon,
Nor a bath, nor ointment, nor flowers,
Nor well-adorned hair.
Only perfectly cultivated speech
Thoroughly adorns a man.
All adornments fade away always.
Adornment of speech is the real adornment.*

Learning is decidedly man's superior mark.
It is wealth hidden and disguised.
Learning brings material pleasures.
Learning brings happiness and renown.
Learning is the teacher of teachers.
Learning is a friend on a foreign trip.
Learning is the supreme deity.
Learning is honored by kings, not wealth.
A man who has no learning is a beast.

Kṣāntiś cet, kavacena kiṃ? kim aribhiḥ,
krodho 'sti ced dehināṃ?
jñātiś ced, analena kiṃ? yadi suhṛd,
divy'|âuṣadhaiḥ kiṃ phalam?
kiṃ sarpair, yadi durjanāḥ? kim u dhanair,
vidy"|ânavadyā yadi?
vrīḍā cet, kim u bhūṣaṇaiḥ? sukavitā
yady asti, rājyena kim?

Dākṣiṇyaṃ sva|jane, dayā parijane,
śāṭhyaṃ sadā durjane,
prītiḥ sādhu|jane, nayo nṛpa|jane,
vidvaj|jane c' ârjavam,
śauryaṃ śatru|jane, kṣamā guru|jane,
kāntā|jane dhṛṣṭatā,
ye c' âivaṃ puruṣāḥ kalāsu kuśalās
teṣv eva loka|sthitiḥ.

Jāḍyaṃ dhiyo harati, siñcati vāci satyaṃ,
mān'|ônnatiṃ diśati, pāpam apākaroti,
cetaḥ prasādayati, dikṣu tanoti kīrtiṃ
sat|saṅgatiḥ, kathaya, kiṃ na karoti puṃsām?

20 Jayanti te sukṛtino
rasa|siddhāḥ kav'|īśvarāḥ,
n' âsti teṣāṃ yaśaḥ|kāye
jarā|maraṇa|jaṃ bhayam.

If men have patience, what is the need of armor?
If anger, what of enemies?
If a kinsman, what of fire?
If a good friend, what of celestial herbs?
If villains, what of a snake?
If impeccable knowledge, what of wealth?
If modesty, what of adornments?
If talent in poetry, what of a kingdom?

Consideration toward kinsmen, kindness toward servants,
Constant cunning toward a rogue,
Affection toward a good man, prudent policy toward a king,
Honesty toward a wise man,
Valor toward an enemy, patience toward a teacher,
Boldness toward a lovely woman,
Men expert in such arts,
Through them alone is society sustained.*

It removes dullness from the intellect,
Showers truth on one's word,
Confers high respect,
Destroys evil,
Clarifies the mind,
Extends fame everywhere.
Such is association with the good.
Tell me! What does it not do for men?

Victorious and auspicious
The lordly poets perfect in poetic taste.
Their body—fame—has no
Fear born of old age and death.

Kṣut|kṣāmo 'pi jarā|kṛśo 'pi śithila|
    prāyo 'pi kaṣṭāṃ daśāṃ
āpanno 'pi vipanna|dīdhitir api
    prāṇeṣu naśyatsv api
matt'|êbh'|êndra|vibhinna|kumbha|piśita|
    grās'|âika|baddha|spṛhaḥ
kiṃ jīrṇaṃ tṛṇam atti māna|mahatām
    agre|saraḥ kesarī?

Svalpa|snāyu|vas"|âvaseka|malinaṃ
    nirmāṃsam apy asthi goḥ
śvā labdhvā paritoṣam eti, na ca tat
    tasya kṣudhā|śāntaye;
siṃho jambukam aṅkam āgatam api
    tyaktvā nihanti dvipaṃ;
sarvaḥ kṛcchra|gato 'pi vāñchati janaḥ
    sattv'|ânurūpaṃ phalam.

Lāṅgūla|cālanam adhaś caraṇ'|âvaghātaṃ
bhūmau nipatya vadan'|ôdara|darśanaṃ ca
śvā piṇḍadasya kurute; gaja|puṅgavas tu
dhīraṃ vilokayati cāṭuśataiś ca bhuṅkte.

Parivartini saṃsāre
    mṛtaḥ ko vā na jāyate?
sa jāto yena jātena
    yāti vaṃśaḥ samunnatim.

Though emaciated by hunger, though thin with age,
Though enfeebled, though fallen into a desperate state,
Though his splendor is lost,
Though his life is passing away,
Still, greedily intent on one mouthful
Of flesh from the frontal lobe of a powerful rutting
elephant,
Will he eat withered grass,
Walking first among those of great pride, the lion?

Having found a fleshless cow bone,
Filthily dotted with just a little fat and sinew,
A dog is overjoyed, though this does not
Appease his hunger.
A jackal may be nearby, yet a lion
Abandons it, kills an elephant.
His lot may be difficult, yet every man desires
A result befitting his character.

Wags its tail,
Paws at the ground,
Falls to the earth
Shows its face and belly,
The dog for the man giving it a scrap.
But the bull elephant,
Watches gravely,
Eats only after a hundred entreaties.

In this swirling transient existence
What man who has died is not born?
He is really born by whose birth
His lineage becomes exalted.

25 Kusuma|stabakasy' êva
dvayī vṛttir manasvinaḥ:
mūrdhni vā sarva|lokasya,
śīryate vana eva vā.

Santy anye 'pi Bṛhaspati|prabhṛtayaḥ
saṃbhāvitāḥ pañcaṣāḥ.
tān praty eṣa viśeṣa|vikrama|rucī
Rāhur na vairāyate.
dvāv eva grasate Divākara|Niśā|
prāṇ'|ēśvarau bhāsvarau.
bhrātaḥ parvaṇi, paśya, Dānava|patiḥ
śīrṣ"|âvaśeṣ'|ākṛtiḥ.

Vahati bhuvana|
śreṇiṃ Śeṣaḥ phaṇā|phalaka|sthitāṃ,
Kamaṭha|patinā
madhye|pṛṣṭhaṃ sadā sa ca dhāryate,
tam api kurute
kroḍ'|ādhīnaṃ payo|dhir anādarād:
ahaha mahatāṃ
niḥsīmānaś caritra|vibhūtayaḥ.

Varaṃ prāṇ'|ôcchedaḥ
sa|mada|Maghavan|mukta|kuliśa|
prahārair udgacchad|
bahula|dahan'|ôdgāra|gurubhiḥ
tuṣār'|âdreḥ sūnor,
ahaha, pitari kleśa|vivaśe
na c' âsau saṃpātaḥ
payasi payasāṃ patyur ucitaḥ.

As for a flower cluster 25
For a reflective man two lifestyles are possible:
To be at the head of all people
Or just to wither in the forest.

Like Jupiter,
Five or six others are also venerated.
Toward them, and delighting in valor spectacular,
Rahu shows no hostility.
Only these two shining lights he swallows:
Sun, the day-maker, and Moon, lord of night.
At which time, behold, brother!
The Lord of the Dánavas is merely a head.*

This line of worlds Shesha carries,
On the flat of his hood placed.
By the Lord of tortoises on the middle of his back
Is he constantly supported.
Him too the ocean
Effortlessly rests on his own chest.
Surely, the wondrous feats
Of the great are without limit.

Better the death—
By blows from arrogant Indra's loosened thunderbolt
Its unbearable blows, belching flames
Bursting forth thickly—
Of Himálaya's son than,
Alas, with his father overwhelmed by pain,
His quite improper fall
Into the lordly ocean's water.*

Yad acetano 'pi pādaiḥ
spṛṣṭaḥ prajvalati Savitur ina|kāntaḥ,
tat tejasvī puruṣaḥ
para|kṛta|nikṛtiṃ kathaṃ sahate?

30 Siṃhaḥ śiśur api nipatati
mada|malina|kapola|bhittiṣu gajeṣu:
prakṛtir iyaṃ sattvavatāṃ,
na khalu vayas tejasāṃ hetuḥ.

Jātir yātu rasā|talaṃ, guṇa|gaṇas
tatr' âpy adho gacchatāṃ,
śīlaṃ śaila|taṭāt patatv, abhijanaḥ
saṃdahyatāṃ vahninā.
śaurye vairiṇi vajram āśu nipatatv,
artho 'stu naḥ kevalaṃ!
yen' âikena vinā guṇās tṛṇa|lava|
prāyāḥ samastā ime.

Yasy' âsti vittaṃ, sa naraḥ kulīnaḥ,
sa paṇḍitaḥ, sa śrutavān, guṇajñaḥ,
sa eva vaktā, sa ca darśaṇīyaḥ:
sarve guṇāḥ kāñcanam āśrayanti.

When even an insensate sun-stone
Blazes up when touched by the Sun's feet,
How can a man of character
Tolerate abuse from others?

Even as a cub a lion falls upon 30
Elephants, solid cheeks soiled with rut.
This is the nature of the courageous.
Indeed, age is not a cause of valor.

Let lineage go to hell.
Let good qualities go even lower.
Let morality fall off the mountainside.
Let good breeding be consumed in the fire.
Let a thunderbolt instantly fall on valor against the enemy.
Let us only have money.
Without that alone,
All these qualities together are worth a blade of grass.

Any man who is wealthy is of good family,
He is wise, learned, a connoisseur.
He alone is eloquent and he is handsome.
All qualities depend on gold.

Daurmantryān nṛpatir vinaśyati, yatiḥ
saṅgāt, suto lālanād,
vipro 'nadhyayanāt, kulaṃ ku|tanayāc,
chīlaṃ khal'|ôpāsanāt,
hrīr madyād, anavekṣaṇād api kṛṣiḥ,
snehaḥ pravās'|āśrayān,
maitrī c' âpraṇayāt, samṛddhir anayāt,
tyāgāt pramādād dhanam.

Dānaṃ, bhogo, nāśas
tisro gatayo bhavanti vittasya;
yo na dadāti na bhuṅkte,
tasya tṛtīyā gatir bhavati.

35 Maṇiḥ śāṇ'|ôllīḍhaḥ,
samara|vijayī heti|dalitaḥ,
mada|kṣīṇo nāgaḥ,
śaradi sarid|āśyāna|pulinā,
kalā|śeṣaś candraḥ,
surata|mṛditā bāla|vanitā:
tanimnā śobhante;
galita|vibhavāś c' ârthiṣu narāḥ.

Parikṣīṇaḥ kaś cit
spṛhayati yavānāṃ prasṛtaye.
sa paścāt sampūrṇaḥ
kalayati Dharitrīṃ tṛṇa|samām.
ataś c' ânekântyād
guru|laghutay" ârtheṣu dhaninām
avasthā vastūni
prathayati ca saṃkocayati ca.

By bad advice is a king ruined,
By attachment an ascetic, by indulgence a son,
By lack of study a brahmin, by a bad son a family,
By association with rogues good conduct,
By recklessness modesty, by lack of attention agriculture,
By absence from home familial love,
By lack of affection friendship,
By imprudence prosperity, by profligate generosity
wealth.

Generosity, enjoyment, loss
Are the three wayswealth can go.
Whoever neither gives nor consumes
Goes the third way.

A jewel polished on a grindstone, 35
A man victorious in battle pierced by a weapon,
An elephant weakened by flow of rut,
Riverbanks dried up in autumn,
A sickle moon,
A girl languid from lovemaking.
Are all lovely in their decline,
As are men whose wealth has trickled away to suppliants.

An extremely poor man
Is desperate for a handful of barley.
Later, entirely filled up,
He reckons the whole Earth a piece of grass.
So because of the indeterminacy
Of the importance or unimportance of possessions,
It is the circumstances of their owners
which magnifies and diminishes objects.

Rājan, dudhukṣasi yadi Kṣiti|dhenum enāṃ,
ten' âdya vatsam iva lokam amuṃ puṣāṇa;
tasmiṃś ca samyag aniśaṃ paripuṣyamāṇe
nānā|phalaṃ phalati kalpa|lat" êva Bhūmiḥ.

Saty" ânṛtā ca, paruṣā priya|vādinī ca,
hiṃsrā dayālur api c', ârtha|parā vadānyā
nitya|vyayā pracura|nitya|dhan'|āgamā ca:
vār'âṅgan" êva nṛpa|nītir aneka|rūpā.

Ājñā, kīrtiḥ, pālanaṃ brāhmaṇānāṃ,
dānaṃ, bhogo, mitra|saṃrakṣaṇaṃ ca:
yeṣām ete ṣaḍ guṇā na pravṛttāḥ,
ko 'rthas teṣāṃ pārthiv'|ôpāśrayeṇa?

40 Yad Dhātrā nija|bhāla|paṭṭa|likhitaṃ
stokaṃ mahad vā dhanaṃ,
tat prāpnoti maru|sthale 'pi nitarāṃ,
Merau ca n' âto 'dhikam.
tad dhīro bhava! vittavatsu kṛpaṇāṃ
vṛttiṃ vṛthā mā kṛthāḥ,
kūpe, paśya, payo|nidhāv api ghaṭo
gṛhṇāti tulyaṃ jalam.

Akaruṇatvam, akāraṇa|vigrahaḥ,
para|dhane para|yoṣiti ca spṛhā,
sujana|bandhu|janeṣv asahiṣṇutā:
prakṛti|siddham idaṃ hi durātmanām.

King, if you want to milk this Earth as a cow,
Then right now nourish the populace like a calf.
When it is fully nourished always
The Earth, like a tree of plenty, will yield many fruits.

Truthful and lying, harsh speech and flattery,
Violence and compassion, parsimony and generosity,
Always turning over vast amounts of money.
Like a courtesan is the shifting appearance of a king's conduct.

Authority, fame, protection of the brahmins,
Giving, material pleasures, supporting friends.
In those in whom these six qualities are not manifest
Why place reliance, king?

Since the Arranger has written on one's forehead
One's wealth, great or small,
One is bound to acquire that even in a desert,
And no more on Mount Meru.*
So, be steadfast! Toward the wealthy
Don't behave wretchedly for nothing.
Consider! In a well or in the sea a pot
Draws an equal amount of water.

No compassion, fighting without reason,
Coveting others' wealth and others' women,
Intolerance toward good people and kinsmen.
This is the natural condition of evil men.

Durjanaḥ parihartavyo
vidyay" âlaṃkṛto 'pi san;
maṇinā bhūṣitaḥ sarpaḥ
kim asau na bhayaṃ|karaḥ?

Jāḍyaṃ hrīmati gaṇyate, vrata|śucau
dambhaḥ, śucau kaitavaṃ,
śūre nirghṛṇatā, munau vimatitā,
dainyaṃ priy'|ālāpini,
tejasviny avaliptatā, mukharatā
vaktary, aśaktiḥ sthire.
tat ko nāma guṇo bhavet sa guṇināṃ,
yo durjanair n' âṅkitaḥ?

Lobhaś ced aguṇena kiṃ? piśunatā
yady asti kiṃ pātakaiḥ?
satyaṃ cet tapasā ca kiṃ? śuci mano
yady asti tīrthena kim?
saujanyaṃ yadi kiṃ janena? mahimā
yady asti kiṃ maṇḍanaiḥ?
sad|vidyā yadi kiṃ dhanair? apayaśo
yady asti kiṃ mṛtyunā?

45 Śaśī divasa|dhūsaro,
galita|yauvanā kāminī,
saro vigata|vārijaṃ,
mukham an|akṣaraṃ sv|ākṛteḥ,
prabhur dhana|parāyaṇaḥ,
satata|durgatiḥ saj|janaḥ,
nṛp'|âṅgaṇa|gataḥ khalo:
manasi sapta śalyāni me.

A wicked man must be shunned,
Even one embellished with learning.
A snake is adorned with a jewel.*
Is it not frightful?

When someone is modest he is reckoned as dull,
Firm in vows as hypocritical, pure as fraudulent,
Heroic as cruel, thoughtful as stupid,
Speaking amiably as whining,
Dignified as arrogant,
Eloquent as loquacious, being firm as impotent.
Is there any quality of people with good qualities
That will not be besmirched by bad men?

If one is avaricious what matter bad qualities?
If malicious what matter evil deeds?
If true what matter austerities?
If pure in mind what matters pilgrimage?
If benevolent what matters a retinue?
If magnanimous what matters adornment?
If truly learned what matters wealth?
If infamous what matters death?

The moon murky during the day, 45
A passionate woman, whose youth has waned,
A lake bereft of lotuses,
A handsome man's face without eloquence,
A king infatuated with wealth,
A good man constantly in trouble,
A rogue in a royal court.
These are seven spikes in my heart.

Na kaścic caṇḍa|kopānām
　　ātmīyo nāma bhū|bhujām;
hotāram api juhvānaṃ
　　spṛṣṭo dahati pāvakaḥ.

Maunān mūkaḥ, pravacana|paṭur
　　vācako jalpako vā,
dhṛṣṭaḥ pārśve bhavati ca vasan
　　dūrato 'py apragalbhaḥ,
kṣāntyā bhīrur, yadi na sahate
　　prāyaśo n' âbhijātaḥ:
sevā|Dharmaḥ parama|gahano
　　yoginām apy agamyaḥ.

Udbhāsit'|âkhila|khalasya, viśṛṅkhalasya,
prodgāḍha|vismṛta|nij'|âdhama|karma|vṛtteḥ,
daivād avāpta|vibhavasya, guṇa|dviṣo 'sya
nīcasya gocara|gataiḥ sukham āsyate kaiḥ?

Ārambha|gurvī kṣayiṇī krameṇa,
laghvī purā vṛddhimatī ca paścāt,
dinasya pūrv'|ârdha|par'|ârdha|bhinnā:
chāy" êva maitrī khala|saj|janānām.

Nobody is truly intimate
With kings of fiery anger.
If touched,
A fire burns even a sacrificing priest.

By staying quiet he is considered dumb, if skilled in speech
He is loquacious or a prattler.
He is overbearing if too close, but staying his distance
He is timid.
If patient he is cowardly, if impatient
He is generally lacking in breeding.
The Law of service is utterly mysterious,
Incomprehensible even to yogins.

He promotes all the rogues,
Is reckless,
From his own low actions now entirely forgotten
Has his conduct resulted,
His wealth was acquired due to fate,
He hates good qualities.
Within the range of such a boor
Could anyone be happy?

Heavy to begin with, weakening steadily;
Slight at first, then later expansive;
Different as the first half and the second half of the day,
The friendship of rogues and that of good men and
are like shadows.*

50 Mṛga|mīna|saj|janānāṃ
tṛṇa|jala|saṃtoṣa|vihita|vṛttīnām
lubdhaka|dhīvara|piśunā
niṣkāraṇam eva vairiṇo jagati.

Vāñchā saj|jana|saṃgatau, para|guṇe
prītir, gurau namratā,
vidyāyāṃ vyasanaṃ, sva|yoṣiti ratir,
lok'|âpavādād bhayam,
bhaktiḥ Śūlini, śaktir ātma|damane,
saṃsarga|muktiḥ khalaiḥ:
ete yeṣu vasanti nirmala|guṇās,
tebhyo mahadbhyo namaḥ.

Vipadi dhairyam, ath' âbhyudaye kṣamā,
sadasi vāk|paṭutā, yudhi vikramaḥ,
yaśasi c' âbhiratir, vyasanaṃ Śrutau:
prakṛti|siddham idaṃ hi mah"|ātmanām.

Kare ślāghyas tyāgaḥ,
śirasi guru|pāda|praṇayitā,
mukhe satyā vāṇī,
vijayi|bhujayor vīryam atulam,
hṛdi svacchā vṛttiḥ,
Śrutam adhigataṃ ca śravaṇayoḥ:
vin" âpy aiśvaryeṇa
prakṛti|mahatāṃ maṇḍanam idam.

Deer, fish and good men,
Their designated sustenance grass, water and
contentment.
Hunters, fishermen and slanderers
Hostile to them without reason in this world.

To mix with good men—desire, in others' qualities—
Delight, toward one's teacher—humility,
In learning—complete absorption,
with his own wife—lovemaking,
Of criticism by people—fear.
To Shiva—devotion, in self-control—strength.
Of association with rogues—avoidance.
Men in whom such flawless qualities dwell,
To those great men—obeisance.

Fortitude in misfortune, patience in success,
Eloquence in the assembly hall, valor in battle,
Delight in fame, total absorption in the Vedas.
These are acquired naturally by great men.

For the hand generosity is praiseworthy,
For the head obeisance at a teacher's feet,
For the mouth truth in speech,
For victorious arms unequalled strength,
For the heart clarity in conduct,
For the ears Vedic learning.
Even without wealth
This is an adornment of those naturally great.

Prāṇ'|āghātān nivṛttiḥ, para|dhana|haraṇe,
saṃyamaḥ, satyavākyaṃ,
kāle śaktyā pradānaṃ, yuvati|jana|kathā|
mūka|bhāvaḥ pareṣām,
tṛṣṇā|sroto|vibhaṅgo, guruṣu ca vinayaḥ,
sarva|bhūt'|ânukampā|sāmānyaṃ:
sarva|śāstreṣv anupahata|vidhiḥ
śreyasām eṣa panthāḥ.

55 Saṃpatsu mahatāṃ cittaṃ
bhaved utpala|komalam,
āpatsu ca mahā|śaila|
śilā|saṃghāta|karkaśam.

Priyā nyāyyā vṛttir,
malinam asu|bhaṅge 'py asukaraṃ,
tv asanto n' âbhyarthyāḥ,
suhṛd api na yācyaḥ kṛśa|dhanaḥ,
vipady uccaiḥ sthairyaṃ,
padam anuvidheyaṃ ca mahatāṃ:
satāṃ ken' ôddiṣṭaṃ
viṣamam asi|dhārā|vratam idam?

Cessation from killing, restraint from stealing,
Speaking the truth,
Timely generosity according to capacity,
Silence during gossip about other men's women.
Destruction of the stream of craving, respect toward the
venerable,
Equal compassion toward all beings.
This rule never infringed in all the learned
treatises,
Is the path to the highest goals.

In success the mind of the great 55
Will be soft as the blue lotus.
In distress hard as a great mountain
When it is struck by a rock.

Value right conduct,
Act not in a vile way even at the risk of death,
Make not requests of bad people,
Beg not from a poor man, even if a friend,
In distress stay resolute,
Follow the footsteps of the great.
Who taught this to the good?
It is as difficult as the vow of the sword blade.*

Pradānaṃ pracchannaṃ,
gṛham upagate saṃbhrama|vidhiḥ,
priyaṃ kṛtvā maunaṃ,
sadasi kathanaṃ c' âpy upakṛteḥ,
anutseko lakṣmyā,
nir|abhibhava|sārāḥ para|kathāḥ:
satāṃ ken' ôddiṣṭaṃ
viṣamam asi|dhārā|vratam idam?

Saṃtapt'|âyasi saṃsthitasya payaso
nām' âpi na śrūyate,
mukt'|ākāratayā tad eva nalinī|
patra|sthitaṃ dṛśyate,
antaḥ sāgara|śukti|madhya|patitam
tan mauktikaṃ jāyate:
prāyeṇ'|âdhama|madhyam'|ôttama|juṣām
evaṃvidhā vṛttayaḥ.

Yaḥ prīṇayet sucaritaiḥ pitaraṃ, sa putraḥ,
yad bhartur eva hitam icchati, tat kalatram,
tan mitram, āpadi sukhe ca samakriyaṃ yad:
etat trayaṃ jagati puṇya|kṛto labhante.

Generosity concealed,
Quick to welcome a guest at home,
Keeping good deeds silent,
Extolling in the assembly hall favors received,
Not arrogant with success,
Not boasting when talking of others.
Who taught this to the good?
It is difficult as the vow of the sword blade.

Of water placed on heated iron,
Even the name is not heard of.
On a lotus leaf that same water
Looks like a pearl.
Fallen inside the hollow of a seashell,
A pearl it becomes.
Of those with qualities good, middling or bad
Such are the activities.

Whoever pleases his father with good acts is a son.
Whoever seeks only her husband's benefit is a wife.
A friend acts identically in distress or good circumstances.
The meritorious meet with these three in this world.

60 Namratven' ônnamantaḥ, para|guṇa|kathanaiḥ
svān guṇān khyāpayantaḥ,
sv'|ârthān saṃpādayanto, vitata|pṛthutar'|
ārambha|yatnāḥ par'|ârthe,
kṣānty" âiv' ākṣepa|rūkṣ'|âkṣara|mukhara|mukhān
durjanān duḥkhayantaḥ:
santaḥ sāścarya|caryā jagati bahumatāḥ
kasya n' âbhyarcanīyāḥ?

Bhavanti namrās taravaḥ phal'|ôdgamaiḥ,
nav'|âmbubhir dūra|vilambino ghanāḥ,
anuddhatāḥ sat|puruṣāḥ samṛddhibhiḥ:
svabhāva ev' âiṣa par'|ôpakāriṇām.

Śrotraṃ śruten' âiva, na kuṇḍalena,
dānena pāṇir, na tu kaṅkaṇena,
vibhāti kāyaḥ karuṇ"|ākulānāṃ
par'|ôpakāreṇa, na candanena.

Padm'|ākaraṃ dina|karo vikacaṃ karoti,
candro vikāsayati kairava|cakravālam,
n' âbhyarthito jaladharo 'pi jalaṃ dadāti:
santaḥ svayaṃ para|hite vihit'|âbhiyogāḥ.

By bowing they are uplifted, by praising others' qualities 60
They proclaim their own good qualities.
In promoting their own goals, they constantly and
expansively
Strive to achieve others' goals.
By their very patience, evil people
who keep mouthing rough words of abuse
They annoy.
The good behave so amazingly in the world, highly
respected are they.
Who would not honor them?

Bowed are the trees with ripening fruit
Hang low the clouds with new water.
Humbled are good men by success
This is certainly the intrinsic nature of those helping
others.

Of people filled with compassion,
Only through learning does the ear shine, not by an
earring.
Through generosity the hand, but not by gold.
The body, through doing good for others,
Not by sandalwood ointment.

The sun makes brilliantly resplendent the lotus grove,
The moon makes the profusion of white night lotuses
bloom,
Though unasked the cloud too gives water.
Spontaneously the good apply themselves to others'
benefit.

Ete sat|puruṣāḥ, par'|ârtha|ghaṭakāḥ
sv'|ârthān parityajya ye;
sāmānyās tu, par'|ârtham udyama|bhṛtaḥ
sv'|ârth'|âvirodhena ye;
te 'mī mānuṣa|rākṣasāḥ, para|hitaṃ
sv'|ârthāya nighnanti ye;
ye tu ghnanti nirarthakaṃ para|hitaṃ,
tan kena jānīmahe?

65 Pāpān nivārayati, yojayate hitāya,
guhyaṃ nigūhati, guṇān prakaṭī|karoti,
āpad|gataṃ ca na jahāti, dadāti kāle:
san|mitra|lakṣaṇam idaṃ pravadanti santaḥ.

Kṣīreṇ' ātma|gat'|ôdakāya hi guṇā
dattāḥ purā te 'khilāḥ,
kṣīr'|ôttāpam avekṣya tena payasā
sv'|ātmā kṛśānau hutaḥ,
gantuṃ pāvakam unmanas tad abhavad
dṛṣṭvā tu mitr'|āpadaṃ,
yuktaṃ tena jalena śāmyati: satāṃ
maitrī punas tv īdṛśī.

Itaḥ svapiti Keśavaḥ, kulam itas tadīya|dviṣām,
itaś ca śaraṇ'|ârthinaḥ śikhariṇāṃ gaṇāḥ śerate,
ito 'pi vaḍav'|ânalaḥ saha samasta|saṃvartakaiḥ:
aho vitatam ūrjitaṃ bhara|sahaṃ ca sindhor vapuḥ

Noble men strive to accomplish others' goals,
Their own goals completely they leave.
Middling men exert themselves for the others' goals
When consistent with their own goals.
Those human demons, for their own benefit
Of others' good destructive are.
But those who pointlessly destroy the others' benefit,
Them how can we understand?

From evil he holds back, applies himself to good, 65
A secret he keeps, good qualities he publicizes,
He abandons not a man in distress, he is generous at the right time.
Such is the mark of a true friend, declare the good.

To the water within it
The milk firstly gave all its own qualities.
The water seeing the milk's overheating
Offered itself into the fire.
The milk became eager to go to the fire
On seeing its friend's distress.
Mixed with the water it is calmed.
Such is the friendship of the good.*

Here sleeps Vishnu,
There his mass of enemies,
Here seeking refuge
The hosts of winged-mountains lie.
There the submarine fire
With all its fires of cosmic destruction.
Behold in its strength and extent
The burden-bearing body of the ocean!

Jātaḥ kūrmaḥ sa ekaḥ pṛthu|bhuvana|bharāy'
ârpitaṃ yena pṛṣṭhaṃ,
ślāghyaṃ janma Dhruvasya bhramati niyamitaṃ
yatra tejasvi|cakram,
saṃjāta|vyartha|pakṣāḥ para|hita|karaṇe
n' ôpariṣṭān na c' âdhaḥ,
Brahm"|âṇḍ'|ôdumbar'|ânto maśakavad apare
jantavo jāta|naṣṭāḥ.

Tṛṣṇāṃ chindhi, bhaja kṣamāṃ, jahi madaṃ,
pāpe ratiṃ mā kṛthāḥ,
satyaṃ brūhy, anuyāhi sādhu|padavīṃ,
sevasva vidvaj|janam,
mānyān mānaya, vidviṣo 'py anunaya
prakhyāpaya praśrayaṃ,
kīrtiṃ pālaya, duḥkhite kuru dayām:
etat satāṃ ceṣṭitam.

70 Manasi vacasi kāye
puṇya|pīyūṣa|pūrṇāḥ,
tri|bhuvanam upakāra|
śreṇibhiḥ prīṇayantaḥ,
para|guṇa|param'|âṇūn
parvatī|kṛtya nityaṃ,
nija|hṛdi vikasantaḥ khyāpayantaḥ kiyantaḥ?

Born was that tortoise unique
Who for the burden of the wide world offered his back.
Praiseworthy the birth of the Pole Star
On whom is anchored the circle of revolving luminaries.
Rendered useless, were the wings of other creatures
For helping others whether above or below them,
They live and die in Brahma's egg,*
Like mosquitoes on a fig tree.

Cut away craving, maintain patience, give up arrogance,
Do not delight in evil,
Speak the truth, follow the path of the good,
Honor learned men,
Praise those worthy of praise, conciliate your enemies,
Proclaim your modesty,
Preserve your reputation, be compassionate toward one
distressed.
Such is the behavior of the good.

In thought, word and deed, 70
Filled with the ambrosia of merit,
Delighting the universe
With their strings of good deeds.
Even the atomic virtues of others
They always make into mountains.
And proclaim, beaming in their own hearts.
How many are such people?

Ratnair mah"|âbdhes tutuṣur na devāḥ,
na bhejire bhīma|viṣeṇa bhītim,
sudhāṃ vinā na prayayur virāmaṃ;
na niścit'|ârthād viramanti dhīrāḥ.

Prārabhyate na khalu vighna|bhayena nīcaiḥ,
prārabhya vighna|vihatā viramanti madhyāḥ,
vighnair muhur muhur api pratihanyamānāḥ
prārabdham uttama|guṇā na parityajanti.

Kvacit pṛthvī|śayyaḥ,
    kvacid api ca paryaṅka|śayanaḥ,
kvacic chāk'|āhāraḥ,
    kvacid api ca śāly'|ôdana|ruciḥ,
kvacit kanthā|dhārī,
    kvacid api ca divy'|âmbara|dharaḥ,
manasvī kāry'|ârthī
    na gaṇayati duḥkhaṃ na ca sukham.

Nindantu nīti|nipuṇā, yadi vā stuvantu,
lakṣmīḥ samāviśatu, gacchatu vā yath"|êṣṭam,
ady' âiva vā maraṇam astu, yug'|ântare vā;
nyāyyāt pathaḥ pravicalanti padaṃ na dhīrāḥ.

Jewels from the huge ocean did not satisfy the gods,
They felt no fear of the ferocious poison.
Until they found the ambrosia they did not stop.
From a definite goal the resolute never desist.

Certainly for fear of obstacles the low do not begin;.
Having begun, when struck by obstacles, the middling stop;
Though by obstacles repeatedly struck
What has been begun the highest men never relinquish.

Sometimes his bed is on the ground,
Sometimes he sleeps on a couch.
Sometimes his food is vegetables,
Sometimes choice boiled rice.
Sometimes he wears rags,
Sometimes he is garbed in celestial garments.
The reflective man who seeks to achieve his goal
Reckons neither sorrow nor happiness.

Those skilled in human affairs may criticize
Or give praise.
Wealth may enter
Or leave at will.
Death may occur right now
Or at the end of the cosmic period.
No men of character
Deviate a step from the right path.

75 Kāntā|kaṭākṣa|viśikhā na lunanti yasya
cittaṃ na nirdahati kopa|kṛśānu|tāpaḥ
karṣanti bhūri|viṣayāś ca na lobha|pāśā
loka|trayaṃ jayati kṛtsnam idaṃ sa dhīraḥ.

Kad|arthitasy' âpi ca dhairya|vṛtteḥ
na śakyate dhairya|guṇaḥ pramārṣṭum;
adho|mukhasy' âpi kṛtasya vahneḥ
n' âdhaḥ śikhā yānti kadācid eva.

Varaṃ śṛṅg'|ôtsaṅgād Guru|śikhariṇaḥ kv' âpi viṣame
patitv" âyaṃ kāyaḥ kaṭhina|dṛṣad|ante vigalitaḥ;
varaṃ nyasto hastaḥ phaṇi|pati|mukhe tīkṣṇa|daśane;
varaṃ vahnau pātas tad api na kṛtaḥ śīla|vilayaḥ.

Vahnis tasya jalāyate, jala|nidhiḥ kulyāyate tatkṣaṇān,
Meruḥ svalpa|śilāyate, mṛga|patiḥ sadyaḥ kuraṅgāyate,
vyālo mālya|guṇāyate, viṣa|rasaḥ pīyūṣa|varṣāyate,
yasy' âṅge 'khila|loka|vallabhataraṃ śīlaṃ samunmīlati.

The arrows—glances of young women 75
Do not pierce his mind.
Nor does the heat of anger
Burn it.
Nor do bonds—strong desires
Drag the multifarious objects of the senses to it.
That man of character
Conquers this entire triple-world.

Even if a man of composed conduct is reviled
His quality of composure cannot be effaced.
Even if a fire is turned upside down,
Downward its flames never go.

Better that from the peak
Of Himálaya onto somewhere rough,
This body should have fallen
And come apart on the spur of a rugged rock.
Better my hand be placed
In the sharp-fanged mouth of a cobra.
Better to fall in the fire
Than that good conduct be brought to ruin.

For him—
Fire turns into water
The ocean instantly turns into a ditch
Meru turns into a hillock
A lion instantly turns into a deer
A snake turns into a wreath of flowers
Poison turns into a shower of ambrosia—
In whose body good conduct,
Adored by all the world, unfolds.

Chinno 'pi rohati taruḥ,
kṣīṇo 'py upacīyate punaś candraḥ;
iti vimṛśantaḥ santaḥ
saṃtapyante na viślathyeṣu lokeṣu.

80 Aiśvaryasya vibhūṣaṇaṃ sujanatā,
śauryasya vāk|saṃyamaḥ,
jñānasy' ôpaśamaḥ, śrutasya vinayo,
vittasya pātre vyayaḥ,
akrodhas tapasaḥ, kṣamā prabhavitur,
Dharmasya nirvyājatā;
sarveṣām api sarva|kāraṇam idaṃ
śīlaṃ paraṃ bhūṣaṇam.

Netā yasya Bṛhaspatiḥ, praharaṇaṃ
vajraṃ, surāḥ sainikāḥ,
svargo durgam, anugrahaḥ khalu Harer,
Airāvaṇo vāraṇaḥ.
ity āścarya|bal'|ânvito 'pi Bala|bhid
bhagnaḥ paraiḥ saṃgare;
tad vyaktaṃ nanu daivam eva śaraṇaṃ.
dhig! dhig! vṛthā pauruṣam.

Bhagn'|āśasya karaṇḍa|piṇḍita|tanor
mlān'|êndriyasya kṣudhā
kṛtv" ākhur vivaraṃ svayaṃ nipatito
naktaṃ mukhe bhoginaḥ.
tṛptas tat|piśitena satvaram asau
ten' âiva yātaḥ pathā.
svasthās tiṣṭhata! daivam eva hi paraṃ
vṛddhau kṣaye kāraṇam.

Though cut, still grows a tree,
Though diminished, waxes once more the moon.
Considering this, the good
Suffer no distress from people lax in their duty.

Of royalty amiability is the adornment 80
Of heroism moderation in speech
Of knowledge calmness, of learning humility,
Of wealth well-directed generosity
Of austerity absence of anger, of capability patience
Of the Law sincerity
Of all these the entire cause
Is good conduct, a supreme adornment.

Brihas·pati was his guide, the thunderbolt his weapon,
The gods his soldiers,
Heaven his fort, Vishnu favored him,
His elephant Airávana.
Though extraordinarily strong, Bala's killer
Was still defeated in battle by his enemies.
Clearly one's only refuge is fate.
Damn! Damn! The uselessness of valor.

In the night a mouse made an opening
And fell by itself into the mouth of a snake
Hopes crushed, body coiled in a box,
Faculties weakened by hunger.
Satiated by his flesh
He left quickly by that very route.
Stand confident! Because fate alone
Is the supreme cause of increase and decline.

Yathā kanduka|pāten' ôt-
patаty āryaḥ patann api;
tathā tv anāryaḥ patati
mṛt|piṇḍa|patanaṃ yathā.

Khalvāṭo divas'|ēśvarasya kiraṇaiḥ
saṃtāpite mastake
gacchan deśam anātapaṃ druta|gatis
tālasya mūle sthitaḥ.
tatr' âpy asya mahā|phalena patatā
bhagnaṃ sa|śabdaṃ śiraḥ.
prāyo gacchati yatra daiva|hatakas,
tatr' âiva yānty āpadaḥ.

85 Gaja|bhujaṅga|vihaṅgama|bandhanaṃ,
śaśi|divākarayor graha|pīḍanam,
matimatāṃ ca nirīkṣya daridratāṃ
«vidhir aho balavān! iti» me matiḥ.

Sṛjati tāvad aśeṣa|guṇ'|ākaraṃ
puruṣa|ratnam alaṅkaraṇaṃ Bhuvaḥ,
tad api tat|kṣaṇa|bhaṅgi karoti ced;
ahaha kaṣṭam, apaṇḍitatā Vidheḥ!

Like a falling ball
A noble man may fall
But bounces back.
But
Like a falling clod of earth
An ignoble man
Just falls.

A bald-headed man,
His head scorched by the sun's rays,
Hastening to a shady spot,
Stood at the foot of a palm tree.
And there, by a large falling fruit
His head was split open with a crack.
Generally where the victim of fate goes
There disastes follow him.

The bondage of elephants, snakes and birds, 85
Eclipses of the moon and sun,
And the poverty of intelligent people.
Observing all this it was obvious to me.
"Fate is powerful. Damn!"

First he creates a jewel of a man,
A mine of all good qualities, an adornment of the
  Earth.
If then he also destroys him in an instant,
Woe and alas for Fate's stupidity.

Yen' âiv' *âmbara|khaṇḍena*
saṃvīto niśi candramāḥ,
ten' âiva ca divā bhānur;
aho daurgatyam etayoḥ!

Ayam amṛta|nidhānaṃ,
nāyako 'py oṣadhīnāṃ,
Śata|bhiṣag|anuyātaḥ,
Śaṃbhu|mūrdhno 'vataṃsaḥ,
virahayati na c' âinaṃ
rāja|yakṣmā śaśāṅkaṃ;
hata|vidhi|paripākaḥ
kena vā laṅghanīyaḥ?

Priya|sakha, vipad|daṇḍ'|āghāta|prapāta|paraṃparā|
paricaya|bale cintā|cakre nidhāya vidhiḥ khalaḥ
mṛdam iva balāt piṇḍīkṛtya pragalbha|kulālavad
bhramayati mano; no jānīmaḥ kim atra vidhāsyati.

90 Virama, viram' āyāsād asmād
dur|adhyavasāyataḥ
vipadi mahatāṃ dhairya|dhvaṃsaṃ
yad' īkṣitum īhase;
ayi jaḍa|vidhe! kalp'|âpāye 'py
apeta|nija|kramāḥ
kula|śikhariṇaḥ kṣudrā n' âite
na vā jala|rāśayaḥ.

By the same *piece of the cloth : part of the sky*
As the moon is covered by night,
The sun is by day.
How unfortunate they are!

He is a repository of ambrosia,
King of the herbs,
Followed by the constellation Shata·bhishaj,
The crest on Shambhu's head.
But consumption does not leave him,
The hare-marked moon.
The ripening of evil fate,
Can anything thwart it?

Dear friend! On this wheel of anxiety
Which has the impetus of an accumulating series
Of strikings and poundings by the rod of misfortune,
Fate, the rogue—like a confident potter who has by force
Made a lump of clay into a ball—
Spins my mind.
We don't know
What he will make of it.

Give it up! Give it up! This effort, 90
This foolish perseverance,
The fortitude of the great shattered in a state of distress
If you desire to observe.
Oh! Senseless Fate! Even at the end of a cosmic period,
When their course is run,
Neither the mountain chains
Nor the oceans are diminished.

Daivena Prabhuṇā svayaṃ jagati yad
    yasya pramāṇīkṛtaṃ,
tat tasy' ôpanamen; manāg api mahān
    n' âiv' āśrayaḥ kāraṇam;
sarv'|āśā|paripūrake jala|dhare
    varṣaty api pratyahaṃ,
sūkṣmā eva patanti cātaka|mukhe
    dvi|trāḥ payo|bindavaḥ.
namasyāmo devān,
    nanu hata|vidhes te 'pi vaśagā;
vidhir vandyaḥ so 'pi
    pratiniyata|karm'|âika|phala|daḥ;
phalaṃ karm'āyattaṃ
    yadi, kim aparaiḥ kiṃ ca vidhinā?
namas tat karmabhyo,
    vidhir api na yebhyaḥ prabhavati.*

Brahmā yena kulālavan niyamito
    brahm"|âṇḍa|bhāṇḍ'|ôdare,
Viṣṇur yena daś'|âvatāra|gahane
    kṣipto mahā|saṃkaṭe,
Rudro yena kapāla|pāṇi|puṭake
    bhikṣ"|âṭanaṃ sevate,
Sūryo bhrāmyati nityam eva gagane,
    tasmai namaḥ karmaṇe.

By Lord Fate itself in this world
Is everything apportioned
And to each person distributed. Even a greater protector
Can contribute not even a bit.
When a cloud covering all directions
Rains each day
Only two or three minuscule drops of water
Fall in the mouth of the *chátaka* bird.
We make obeisance to the gods
But they too are subject to evil fate.
So Fate should be praised
Since it gives the fruits only of each particular action.
But if the result depends on the action,
What of others, what of fate?
So obeisance to actions.
Even Fate does not prevail over them.

By which like a potter Brahma is confined
Within the vessel that is his creation.
By which Vishnu is cast into the thicket of the ten
  incarnations
At times of huge distress.
By which Rudra, skull in his cupped hand,
Roams about begging.
By which Surya is made forever to wander in the sky.
Obeisance to karma.

Yā sādhūṃś ca khalān karoti, viduṣo
mūrkhān, hitān dveṣiṇaḥ,
pratyakṣaṃ kurute parokṣam, amṛtaṃ
hālāhalaṃ tat|kṣaṇāt,
tām ārādhaya sat|kriyāṃ bhagavatīṃ
bhoktuṃ phalaṃ vāñchitaṃ.
he sādho! vyasanair guṇeṣu vipuleṣv
āsthāṃ vṛthā mā kṛthāḥ.

Śubhraṃ sadma, sa|vibhramā yuvatayaḥ,
śvet'|ātapatr'|ôjjvalā
lakṣmīr ity anubhūyate ciram anu-
syūte śubhe karmaṇi;
vicchinne nitarām anaṅga|kalaha|
krīḍā|truṭat|tantukaṃ
muktā|jālam iva prayāti jhaṭiti
bhraśyad diśo. dṛśyatām!

95 Guṇavad aguṇavad vā
kurvatā kārya|jālaṃ
pariṇatir avadhāryā
yatnataḥ paṇḍitena;
atirabhasa|kṛtānāṃ
karmaṇām ā|vipatteḥ
bhavati hṛdaya|dāhī
śalya|tulyo vipākaḥ.

She makes the bad good,
Fools intelligent, enemies friends,
Makes the secret open, instantly turns poison into
  ambrosia.
Propitiate her, that goddess—good conduct
If you would enjoy your desired goal.
Good man!
Do not make useless your dependence
On many virtues by having vices.

Splendid home, flirtatious young women,
Blazing white umbrella,
Prosperity. Such are experienced
When goodkarma is strung together over a long time.
When it is utterly destroyed, just as a mass of pearls
Whose thread has broken in the play
Of a love quarrel,
It suddenly disperses to all directions. Consider this!

While doing his round of duties 95
Whether good or not
The consequence should be considered
Carefully by the wise man.
Of actions done impetuously
The result, like a dart,
Burns his heart
Until he dies.

Sthālyāṃ vaiḍūrya|mayyāṃ
    pacati tila|khalaṃcāndanair indhan'|âughaiḥ;
sauvarṇair lāṅgal'|âgrair
    vilikhati vasudhām arka|mūlasya hetoḥ;
chittvā karpūra|khaṇḍān
    vṛttim iha kurute kodravāṇāṃ samantāt:
prāpy' êmāṃ karma|bhūmiṃ
    na bhajati manujo yas tapo manda|bhāgyaḥ.

N' âiv' ākṛtiḥ phalati, n' âiva kulaṃ, na śīlaṃ,
vidy" âpi n' âiva, na ca yatna|kṛt" âpi sevā;
bhāgyāni pūrva|tapasā khalu saṃcitāni
kāle phalanti puruṣasya yath" âiva vṛkṣāḥ.

Majjatv ambhasi, yātu Meru|śikharaṃ,
    śatrūñ jayatv āhave,
vāṇijyaṃ kṛṣi|sevane ca sakalā
    vidyāḥ kalāḥ śikṣatu,
ākāśaṃ vipulaṃ prayātu khagavat;
    kṛtvā prayatnaṃ paraṃ;
n' âbhāvyaṃ bhavat' îha karma|vaśato:
    bhāvyasya nāśaḥ kutaḥ?

In a dish made of topaz jewels
He cooks dregs of sesamum oil on bundles of sandalwood
fuel.
With gold-tipped plowshares
He plows the ground to acquire the *arka*
root.
Splitting camphor fragments
He cultivates *kódrava* grain everywhere.
On reaching this arena for action
The unfortunate human does not practice austerities.*

Appearance certainly does not give results, nor does family,
nor good conduct,
Nor learning, nor even diligent service.
Truly, good fortune accumulated by prior austerities
Bears fruit for a man over time, just like trees.

Let him dive into the water, go to the peak of Meru,
Defeat his enemies in battle,
Learn all the arts and sciences,
Trade, agriculture and service.
Let him traverse the expansive sky like a bird.
By making the utmost effort,
By the power of karma, nothing in this world which is not
to be can be.
How can what is to be come to naught?

Vane, raṇe, śatru|jal'|âgni|madhye,
mah"|ârṇave, parvata|mastake vā,
suptaṃ, pramattaṃ, viṣama|sthitaṃ vā,
rakṣanti puṇyāni purā|kṛtāni.

100 Bhīmaṃ vanaṃ bhavati tasya puraṃ pradhānaṃ,
sarvo janaḥ svajanatām upayāti tasya;
kṛtsnā ca Bhūr bhavati san|nidhi|ratna|pūrṇā
yasy' âsti pūrva|sukṛtaṃ vipulaṃ narasya.

He might be in the forest, in battle amid enemies, fire or
water,
In the great ocean or on a mountain peak.
But prior meritorious deeds protect him
Whether he is asleep, careless or in difficulty.

The terrible jungle becomes his capital city; 100
For him every man becomes an intimate.
The entire Earth becomes full of accessible goods
For the man whose prior good actions are vast.

BHARTRI·HARI: PASSION

Śambhu|Svayaṃbhū|Harayo hariṇ'|ēkṣaṇānām
yen' âkriyanta satataṃ gṛha|kumbha|dāsāḥ,
vācām agocara|caritra|vicitritāya;
tasmai namo bhagavate makara|dhvajāya.

Smitena bhāvena ca lajjayā bhiyā
parāṅ|mukhair ardha|kaṭākṣa|vīkṣaṇaiḥ
vacobhir īrṣyā|kalahena līlayā:
samasta|bhāvaiḥ khalu bandhanaṃ striyaḥ.

Bhrū|cāturyāt
    kuñcit'|âkṣāḥ
snigdhā vāco
    lajjit'|ântāś ca hāsāḥ
līlā|mandaṃ
    prasthitaṃ ca sthitaṃ ca:
strīnām etad
    bhūṣaṇaṃ c' āyudhaṃ ca.

SHIVA, BRAHMA AND VISHNU
Were made always to act
As household slaves
Of doe-eyed women by him,
Whose marvellous actions
Defy words.
Obeisance to him, the Lord
On whose banner is a fish.

With a smile, emotion,
Coyness, fright,
Hostile looks, glances from
Sultry eyes,
Sweet words, jealous
Quarrels and playfulness.
With all these affectations
Is the bondage of woman.

Curvaceous eyes from dancing brows,
Sidelong glances,
Affectionate words,
Smiles ending in coyness,
Playful languor
Movement and stillness.
Of woman,
Here is both ornament and weapon.

Kva cit sa|bhrū|bhaṅgaiḥ
    kva cid api ca lajjā parigataiḥ
kva cid bhūri|trastaiḥ
    kva cid api ca līlā|vilasataiḥ
kumārīṇām etair
    madana|subhagair netra|valitaiḥ
sphuran|nīl'|âbjānāṃ
    prakara|parikīrṇā iva diśaḥ.

5 Vaktraṃ candra|vikāsi, paṅkaja|parī|
    hāsa|kṣame locane,
varṇaḥ svarṇam, apākariṣṇur alinī|
    jiṣṇuḥ kacānāṃ cayaḥ,
vakṣo|jāv ibha|kumbha|vibhrama|harau,
    gurvī nitamba|sthalī,
vācāṃ hāri ca mārdavaṃ yuvatiṣu
    svābhāvikaṃ maṇḍanam.

Smitaṃ kiṃcin mugdhaṃ
    sarala|taralo dṛṣṭi|vibhavaḥ
parispando vācām
    abhinava|vilās'|ôkti|sarasaḥ
gatānām ārambhaḥ
    kisalayita|līlā|parikaraḥ
spṛśantyās tāruṇyaṃ
    kim iva na hi ramyaṃ mṛga|dṛśaḥ?

Here a contraction of lovely brows,
There filled with coyness,
Here heightened alarm,
There flashes of amorous playfulness.
With youthful girls,
Enchanting, darting eyes,
Every direction is seemingly sprinkled with heaps
Of blue lotus bursting forth.

Face outshining the moon,
Eyes capable of deriding the lotus,
Complexion surpassing gold,
Hair excelling the black bee's ebony,
Breasts shifting fascination away from the elephant's
bosses,
Voluptuous hips,
Enchanting and soft of word.
Natural is young women's adornment.

Smile well-nigh beautiful.
The power of her glance, simple and tremulous,
The quivering of her words,
Savoring talk of new diversions,
Contriving movements,
Opulently graceful as a young bud.
Of a doe-eyed woman touching youth,
Is this not the charm?

Draṣṭavyeṣu kim uttamaṃ mṛga|dṛśaḥ.
  prema|prasannaṃ mukham,
ghrātavyeṣv api kiṃ tad|āsya|pavanaḥ,
  śravyeṣu kiṃ tad|vacaḥ,
kiṃ svādyeṣu tad|oṣṭha|pallava|rasaḥ,
  spṛśyeṣu kiṃ tad|vapuḥ,
dhyeyaṃ kiṃ nava|yauvanaṃ sahṛdayaiḥ
  sarvatra tad|vibhramāḥ?

Etāś calad|valaya|saṃhati|mekhal'|ôttha|
jhaṅkāra|nūpura|parā|jita|rāja|haṃsyaḥ
kurvanti kasya na mano vivaśaṃ taruṇyaḥ
vitrasta|mugdha|hariṇī|sadṛśaiḥ kaṭākṣaiḥ?

Kuṅkuma|paṅka|kalaṅkita|dehā
gaura|payo|dhara|kampita|hārā
nūpura|haṃsa|raṇat|pada|padmā
kaṃ na vasī|kurute Bhuvi rāmā?

10 Nūnaṃ hi te kavi|varā viparīta|vācaḥ
ye nityam āhur abalā iti kāminīs tāḥ;
yābhir vilolatara|tāraka|dṛṣṭi|pātaiḥ
Śukr'|ādayo 'pi vijitās tv abalāḥ kathaṃ tāḥ?

Of things seen, what is superior
To the affectionate and serene face of a doe-eyed woman?
Of fragrances, what is superior to the breath of her mouth,
Of sounds, what is superior to her speech?
Of tastes, what is superior to the flavor of her bud-like lips,
Of touch, what is superior to her body?
Need the sophisticate contemplate new youth?
Its graces are everywhere.

Surpassed are the royal swans
By the moving bangles,
The clashing girdles
And tinkling anklets.
Whose mind can these young girls
Fail to render helpless
With a glance from their doe-eyes,
So vulnerable and delicate?

Body stained with *kunkum* paste,
Necklace trembling on white breasts,
Feet of lotuses tinkling like ankleted geese.
Who on Earth does a lovely woman not bring into subjection?

Assuredly excellent poets speak perversely 10
When always they declare sensuous women are truly weak.
By glances from eyes motioning dramatically about
Even Indra and others are defeated. How can they be weak?

Nūnam ājñā|karas tasyāḥ
 subhruvo makara|dhvajaḥ
yatas tan|netra|saṃcāra|
 sūciteṣu pravartate.

Keśāḥ saṃyaminaḥ śruter api paraṃ
 pāraṃ gate locane,
antar|vaktram api svabhāva|śucibhiḥ
 kīrṇaṃ dvijānāṃ gaṇaiḥ,
muktānāṃ satat'|âdhivāsa|rucirau
 vakṣo|ja|kumbhāv imau:
itthaṃ tanvi vapuḥ praśāntam api te
 rāgaṃ karoty eva naḥ!

Mugdhe! dhānuṣkatā k" êyam
 apūrvā tvayi dṛśyate?
yayā vidhyasi cetāṃsi
 guṇair eva, na sāyakaiḥ.

Sati pradīpe, saty agnau,
 satsu tārā|maṇ'|îndusu,
vinā me mṛga|śāv'|âkṣyā
 tamo|bhūtam idaṃ jagat.

Surely, he whose banner contains a fish
Is the servant of a beautiful-browed woman.
Since, according to the gesture of her eyes,
He proceeds.

Hair looped up from the ear
Extends back beyond her eyes,
Her mouth, filled with rows of teeth
White by nature.
A splendid constant abode of pearls
Her two pot-like breasts.
So slender woman! This body of yours
Might be calm, but it impassions us absolutely.

Delicate woman! Who is this archer who has
Not appeared before?
She pierces hearts
But not with arrows: by her graces.

There may be light, may be fire,
May be stars, jewels, the moon.
But without my doe-eyed woman
This world has become utterly dark.

15 Udvṛttaḥ stana|bhāra eṣa tarale
netre cale bhrū|tale
rāg'|âdhiṣṭhitam oṣṭha|pallavam idaṃ
kurvantu nāma vyathām;
saubhāgy'|âkṣara|mālik" êva likhitā
Puṣp'|āyudhena svayam
madhyasth" âpi karoti tāpam adhikaṃ
rom'|āvaliḥ kena sā?

Mukhena candra|kāntena
mahā|nīlaiḥ śiro|ruhaiḥ
pāṇibhyāṃ padma|rāgābhyāṃ
reje ratna|may" îva sā.

Guruṇā stana|bhāreṇa
mukha|candreṇa bhāsvatā
śānaiś carābhyāṃ pādābhyāṃ
reje graha|may" îva sā.

Yāḥ stanau yadi ghanau jaghanaṃ ca hāri
vaktraṃ ca cāru tava cittaḥ kim ākulatvam?
puṇyaṃ kuruṣva yadi teṣu tav' âsti vāñchā;
puṇyair vinā na hi bhavanti samīhit'|ârthāḥ.

Swollen breasts, tremulous eyes,
Arched eyebrows,
Ruled by passion, bud-like lip,
All certainly provoke alarm.
Sketched by the Flower-weapon god himself
As if she were a garland of auspicious syllables.
This line of hair on her belly,
Why does it torment me so?

Her mouth beautiful as the moon, hair deep black,
Her two hands—rubies.
She radiates,
Virtually a star.

Her breasts heavily burdened,
Her moon-like mouth splendid,
Her feet moving gracefully.
She glitters like a star.

Given women,
Firm breasts, enchanting thigh
And a lovely face,
Why your perturbation, mind?
If you are desirous of them,
Do something nice
If you want them,
For without nice things,
No goals are cherished.

Ime tāruṇya|śrī|
nava|parimalāḥ, prauḍha|surata|
pratāpa|prārambhāḥ,
Smara|vijaya|dāna|pratibhuvaḥ
ciraṃ cetaś corā,
abhinava|vikār'|âika|guravaḥ:
vilāsa|vyāpārāḥ
kim api vijayante mṛga|dṛṣām!

20 Raṇaya|madhurāḥ
prem'|ôdārā ras'|āśryatāṃ gatāḥ
phaṇiti|madhurā
mugdha|prāyāḥ prakāśita|saṃmadāḥ
prakṛti|subhagā
visrambh'|ârdrāḥ Smar'|ôdaya|dāyinaḥ
rahasi kim api
svair'|ālāpā haranti mṛgī|dṛśām.

Viśramya viśramya vana|drumāṇām
chāyāsu tanvī vicacāra kācit,
stan'|ôttarīyeṇa kar'|ôddhṛtena
nivārayantī śaśino mayūkhān.

Adarśane darśana|mātra|kāmā,
dṛṣṭvā pariṣvaṅga|sukh'|âika|lolā;
āliṅgitāyāṃ punar āyat'|âkṣyām
āśāsmahe vigrahayor bhedam.

Fresh fragrances of youth's splendor,
Beginnings of the glow
From intense sex,
Surety for signalling Kama's victory,
Forever, stealers of hearts,
Exclusive teachers of fresh youth's transformations.
Sensuous gestures of doe-eyed women,
Victorious somehow!

Sweet through affection,
Enchanting through love, have become the source of taste,
Sweet in speech,
Predominantly naïve, eagerness for sex portrayed,
Beautiful by nature,
Exuding confidence,
Giving profile to Kama.
The willful chatter of doe-eyed women in secret
Is indescribable.

Resting long in a forest grove's shadows,
A slender woman wandered about,
Breast cloth raised in her hand,
Warding off the moon's rays.*

When he does not appear, she desires only to see him.
Seeing, she is eager only for the happiness of his embrace.
When the woman of long eyes is embraced repeatedly,
We yearn for our bodies' unity.

Mālatī śirasi, jṛmbhaṇaṃ mukhe,
candanaṃ vapuṣi kuṅkum'|āvilam,
vakṣasi priyatamā mad'|ālasā:
svarga eṣa pariśiṣṭa āgamaḥ.

Prāṅ mā m" êti manāg anāgata|rasaṃ,
jāt'|âbhilāṣaṃ tataḥ,
sa|vrīḍaṃ tad anu, ślath'|ôdyamam atha,
pradhvasta|dhairyaṃ punaḥ,
prem'|ârdraṃ spṛhaṇīya|nirbhara|rahaḥ
krīḍā|pragalbhaṃ tataḥ:
niḥsaṅg'|âṅga|vikarṣaṇ'|âdhika|sukhaṃ
ramyaṃ kula|strī|ratam.

25 Urasi nipatitānāṃ srasta|dhamillakānām,
mukulita|nayanānāṃ kiṃcid unmīlitānām,
upari|surata|sveda|svinna|gaṇḍa|sthalānām,
adhara|madhu vadhūnāṃ bhāgyavantaḥ pibanti.

Āmīlita|nayanānāṃ
yaḥ surata|raso 'nu saṃvidaṃ bhāti;
mithunair mitho 'vadhāritam
avitatham idam eva Kāma|nirvahaṇam.

On her head jasmine, on her face a blossoming radiance,
On her body sandalwood stained with *kunkum*,
On her breast a slight lustful languidity, utterly lovely.
A piece of heaven has arrived.

At first strong denial, desire hardly come.
Then once desire has arisen,
Afterward, ashamed her effort is relaxed,
As, once more, her resistance is spent.
Overwhelmed with love, bearing her vast yearning in
secret,
Eager then for further love-play.
Intense is the happiness in stroking her body
unrestrained,
Love-play with one's own wife is delightful.

Of women onto whose breast has fallen
Braided hair now loosened,
With half-closed eyes
Almost opening,
Exhausted by excessive love,
Perspiring cheeks,
Their honey lips
Drain those fortunate men.

Of women whose eyes are closed
The taste of lovemaking
Shines after it is experienced.
By those who mutually experience lovemaking
It is definitely known
That it is truly grounded in Kama.

Idam anucitam akramaś ca puṃsām
yad iha jarāsv api mānmathā vikārāḥ;
tad api ca na kṛtaṃ nitambinīnām
stana|patan'|âvadhi jīvitaṃ rataṃ vā

Rājat tṛṣṇ"|âmbu|rāśer na hi jagati gataḥ
    kaścid ev' âvasanām,
ko v" ârtho 'rthaiḥ prabhūtaiḥ sva|vapuṣi galite
    yauvane sānurāge?
gacchāmaḥ sadma tāvad vikasita|kumud'|
    êndīvar'|ālokinīnām
ākramy' ākramya rūpaṃ jhaṭiti na jarayā
    lupyate preyasīnām.

Rāgasy' āgāram ekaṃ
    naraka|śata|mahā|
    duḥkha|saṃprāpti|hetuḥ;
mohasy' ôtpatti|bījaṃ
    jala|dhara|paṭalaṃ
    jñāna|tār'|âdhipasya;
Kandarpasy' âika|mitraṃ
    prakaṭita|vividha|
    spaṣṭa|doṣa|prabandham:
loke 'smin na hy anartha|
    vraja|kula|bhavanaṃ
    yauvanād anyad asti.

For men it is unsuitable and against the flow of things
That in this world even in old age love's agitations they
  experience.
Similarly, for women of voluptuous hips,
Neither a livelihood nor sex should be practiced once
  their breasts sag.

King, to the end of the ocean of craving
Nobody in the world has gone.
Why possess wealth
When from one's own body impassioned youth has flown
  away?
We will go to our own home
Before the beauty, assailed daily,
Is rapidly taken by old age,
Of our wives,
Their eyes fully expanded blue lotus.

An abode of passion,
Cause of huge misery in one hundred hells,
Seed of the beginning of confusion,
Profusion of clouds over the moon that is knowledge,
Kama's special friend,
Continuous line of conspicuous flaws.
In this world no other house holds a collection of useless
  things
Except for youth.

30 Śṛṅgāra|druma|nīrade prasṛmara|
kriḍā|rasa|srotasi
Pradyumna|priya|bāndhave catura|vāṅ|
muktā|phal'|ôdanvati
tanvī|netra|cakora|pārvaṇa|vidhau
saubhāgya|lakṣmī|nidhau
dhanyaḥ ko 'pi na vikriyāṃ kalayati
prāpte nave yauvane?

Saṃsāre 'sminn asāre ku|nṛpati|bhavana|
dvāra|sev"|âvalamba|
vyāsaṅga|dhvasta|dhairyaṃ katham amala|dhiyo
mānasaṃ saṃvidadhyuḥ;
yady etāḥ prodyad|indu|
dyuti|nicaya|bhṛto na syur ambhoja|netrāḥ
preṅkhat|kāñcī|kalāpāḥ stana|bhara|vinaman|
madhya|bhājas taruṇyaḥ?

Siddh'|âdhyāsita|kandare, Hara|vṛṣa|
skandh'|âvarugṇa|drume,
Gaṅgā|dhauta|śilā|tale, Himavataḥ
sthāne sthite śreyasi;
kaḥ kurvīta śiraḥ praṇāma|malinaṃ
mlānaṃ manasvī|janaḥ,
yad vitrasta|kuraṅga|śāva|nayanā
na syuḥ Smar'|âstraṃ striyaḥ?

Saṃsāra! tava paryanta|
padavī na davīyasī,
antarā dustarā, na syur
yadi te madir'|ēkṣaṇāḥ.

A water-giving cloud to the tree of sensuosity, 30
A gushing stream of playfulness,
Kama's beloved kinsman,
An ocean of pearls of clever words,
A full moon to those chakora birds, the eyes of slim girls,
A treasury of fortunate prosperity.
No lucky man fails to welcome the change
When his first youth has arrived.

In this vacuous, transient existence
How could men of clear intellect
Allow their minds' resolve to be distracted
By attachment to serving at the gate of a bad king's palace,
Were it not for young girls' lotus-eyes
Splendid as the newly risen moon,
With girdles of bells tinkling
On slender waists bowed by heavy breasts?

If he were in a cave occupied by *siddhas*,
Near a tree damaged by the shoulder of Shiva's bull,
On a slab of rock purified by the Ganges,
When standing on some splendid spot on Hímavat,
What reflective man would lower his head,
Soiled by bowing
Were it not for women, doe-eyes apprehensive.
Women are Love's weapon.

Transient existence! The path to your end
Would not be so distant,
Your interior so difficult to cross,
Were it not for those women with intoxicating eyes.

Diśo vana|hariṇībhyo
vaṃśa|kāṇḍa|cchavīnām
kavalam upala|koṭi|
chinna|mūlaṃ kuśānām;
Śaka|yuvati|kapol'|
āpāṇḍu|tāmbūla|vallī+
dalam aruṇa|nakh'|âgraiḥ pāṭitaṃ vā vadhūbhyaḥ.

35 Asārāḥ sarve te,
virati|virasāḥ, pāpa|viṣayāḥ.
Jugupsyantāṃ yad vā
nanu sakala|doṣ'|āspadam iti;
tath" âpy etad|bhūmau
nahi para|hitāt puṇyam adhikam,
na c' âsmin saṃsāre
kuvalaya|dṛśo ramyam aparam.

Mātsaryam utsārya, vicārya kāryam,
āryāḥ samaryādam idaṃ vadantu:
sevyā nitambāḥ kimu bhūdharāṇām
uta smara|smera|vilāsinīnām?

To the forest does give
A morsel of *kusha* grass—
Splendid as a shoot of bamboo—
Its root cut with a jewel's edge.
To the young brides give
A leaf from the betel plant—
Pale as a Shaka woman's cheek—
Plucked with the tip of reddened nails.

Without substance are they all, 35
Sense objects—evil and ultimately tasteless.
To be shunned totally
As the abode of all evils.
Even so, in the world
There may be no merit superior to helping others,
Yet in transient existence,
Nothing is superior in delight
To a lotus-eyed woman.

Drive out envy and reflect on the matter.
Then, noble men, declare it precisely.
Should one frequent the slopes of mountains
Or the buttocks of wanton women glistening with lust?

Saṃsāre svapna|sāre pariṇati|tarale
dve gatī paṇḍitānām.
tattva|jñān'|âmṛt'|âmbhaḥ|pluva|lalita|dhiyāṃ
yātu kālaḥ kathaṃcit;
no cen, mugdh'|âṅganānāṃ stana|ghana|jaghan'|
ābhoga|saṃbhoginām
sthūl'|ôpastha|sthalīṣu sthagita|kara|tala|
sparśa|līl"|ôdyamānām.

Āvāsaḥ kṛiyatāṃ Gāṅge
pāpa|hāriṇi vāriṇi.
stana|dvaye taruṇyā vā
mano|hāriṇi hāriṇi.

Kim iha bahubhir uktair
yukti|śūnyaiḥ pralāpaiḥ.
dvayam iha puruṣāṇāṃ
sarvadā sevanīyam.
abhinava|mada|līlā|
lālasaṃ sundarīnām
stana|bhara|parikhinnaṃ
yauvanaṃ vā; vanaṃ vā.

40 Satyaṃ janā vacmi, na pakṣa|pātāl.
lokeṣu saptasv api tathyam etat.
n'|ânyan manohāri nitambinībhyaḥ,
duḥkh'|âika|hetur na ca kaś cid|anyaḥ.

In this dreamy transient existence where any result is
uncertain
There are two paths for the wise.
With minds seeped in the ambrosial liquid of true
knowledge
Time should be diligently spent.
If not, with delicate women, their breasts and firm thighs
Terribly aroused,
Eager for the touch of hands concealed
In realms of ample flesh.

Dwell on the Ganges
Whose water takes away evil.
Or between a young girl's breasts
Whose necklace takes away your mind.

What's the use of garrulous words,
Mere prattle empty of reason.
For men on Earth
Only two lifestyles should be cultivated ever.
Youth, given up to dalliance and the fresh lust
Of beautiful young women
Exhausted by heavy breasts;
Or the forest.

People, I speak the truth, without prejudice.
This is certainly how it is in the seven worlds.
Nothing else is more captivating than women with
beautiful hips
And there is no more profound cause of misery.

Kānt" êty, utpala|locan" êti, vipula|
    śreṇī|bhar" êty, unnamat|
pīn'|ôttuṅga|payodhar" êti, sumukh'|
    âmbhoj" êti, subhrūr iti.
dṛṣṭvā mādyati, modate, 'bhiramate,
    prastauti vidvān api
pratyakṣ'|âśucibhis trikāṃ striyam. aho
    mohasya duśceṣṭitam.

Smṛtā bhavati tāpāya,
    dṛṣṭā c' ônmāda|kāriṇī,
spṛṣṭā bhavati mohāya.
    sā nāma dayitā katham?

Tāvad ev' âmṛta|mayī
    yāval locana|gocarā.
cakṣuḥ|pathād atītā tu
    viṣād apy atiricyate.

N' âmṛtaṃ na viṣaṃ kiṃcid
    ekāṃ muktvā nitambinīm.
s" âiv' âmṛta|latā raktā,
    viraktā viṣa|vallarī.

"Beautiful, lotus-eyes, ample hips,
Large breasts, prominent and elevated,
Bright lotus-like face,
Lovely brow."
Seeing this, he is aroused, blissful, playful,
And sings her praises, even though
The woman's loins are obviously impure.
Alas, the ill-mannered play of ignorance.

Remembered, she conduces to pain.
Seen, evokes excitement.
Touched, conduces to confusion.
How possibly can she be loved?

She is ambrosia
As long as she stays within vision.
Once gone from the eye's path,
Worse than poison.

Nothing is both ambrosia and poison.
Nothing—except for an ample-hipped woman.
Impassioned, the vine of ambrosia,
Without passion, a poisonous creeper.

45 Āvartaḥ saṃśayānām, avinaya|bhuvanaṃ,
pattanaṃ sāhasānām,
doṣānāṃ saṃnidhānaṃ, kapaṭa|śata|mayaṃ,
kṣetram apratyayānām,
svarga|dvārasya vighno, naraka|pura|mukhaṃ,
sarva|māyā|karaṇḍam,
strī|yantraṃ kena sṛṣṭaṃ viṣam amṛta|mayaṃ,
prāṇi|lokasya pāśaḥ.

No satyena mṛg'|âṅka eṣa vadanī|
bhūto, na c' êndīvara|dvandvam
locanatāṃ gataṃ, na kanakair
apy aṅga|yaṣṭiḥ kṛtā.
kiṃ tv evaṃ kavibhiḥ pratārita|manās,
tattvaṃ vijānann api,
tvaṅ|māṃs'|âsthi|mayaṃ vapur mṛga|dṛśāṃ
mando janaḥ sevate.

Līlāvatīnāṃ sahajā vilāsās.
ta eva mūḍhasya hṛdi sphuranti.
rāgo nalinyā hi nisarga|siddhas.
tatra bhramaty eva vṛthā ṣaḍ|aṅghriḥ.

A whirlpool of uncertainties, a world of misconduct, 45
A city of reckless behavior,
A receptacle of faults, embodying one hundred
  deceptions,
A field of distrust,
An obstacle to heaven's door, gateway to hell,
A chamber of every illusion.
Who created this instrument—woman, combining
  poison and ambrosia,
The noose of men.

Truly the moon has not become her face,
Nor two blue lotuses
Transformed into her eyes,
Nor her slender body formed from gold.
But his mind deceived in this way by poets,
Even if still understanding the truth,
The body of doe-eyed women, just skin, flesh and bone,
A stupid man will worship.

Of graceful women flirtatious gestures are innate.
Only in the heart of a fool do they burst forth.
Passion occurs naturally in a lotus.
There only a foolish bee wanders.

Yad etat pūrṇ'|êndu|
        dyuti|haram udār'|ākṛti|param
mukh'|âbjaṃ tanv|aṅgyāḥ,
        kila vasati yatr' âdhara|madhu,
idaṃ tat kiṃ pāka|
        druma|phalam idānīm atirasam.
vyatīte 'smin kāle
        viṣam iva bhaviṣyaty asukhadam.

Unmīlat|tri|valī|taraṅga|nilayā,
        prottuṅga|pīna|stana|
dvandven' ôdgata|cakravāka|yugalā,
        vaktr'|âmbuj'|ôdbhāsinī
kānt"|ākāra|dharā nad" îyam abhitaḥ
        krūr" âtra. n' âpekṣyate
saṃsār'|ârṇava|majjanaṃ yadi,
        tadā dūreṇa saṃtyajyatām.

50 Jalpanti sārdham anyena,
        paśyanty anyaṃ savibhramāḥ,
hṛd|gataṃ cintayanty anyaṃ,
        priyaḥ ko nāma yoṣitām?

Madhu tiṣṭhati vāci yoṣitāṃ,
hṛdi hālāhalam eva kevalam.
ata eva nipīyate 'dharo,
hṛdayaṃ muṣṭibhir eva tāḍyate.

It draws away splendor from the moon,
Utterly lovely in shape,
The slender-bodied woman's lotus-face
Where lips of honey are said to live.
Now it is the fruit of a growing tree,
Its flavor too strong.
When time has passed it will be like poison,
Devoid of pleasure.

The three folds around her waist are its waves,
Her upraised and firm breasts evoke
Its pair of *chakra·vaka* birds taking off,
Her face its glistening lotus.
This river whose form is a woman is everywhere ferocious.
If you yearn not to
Sink into the sea of transient existence,
Abandon her from a distance.

Simultaneously they chatter with one man, 50
Gaze flirtatiously at another,
While in their heart thinking of yet another.
What man is really loved by young women?

Honey stands in the speech of young girls
In their heart poison only.
Therefore the lip only is drunk,
While the heart alone is struck with fists.

Apasara sakhe
dūrād asmāt kaṭākṣa|viṣ'|ânalāt,
prakṛti|viṣamād
yoṣit|sarpād vilāsa|phaṇā|bhṛtaḥ.
itara|phaṇinā
daṣṭaḥ śakyaś cikitsitum auśadhaiḥ.
catura|vanitā|
bhogi|grastaṃ tyajanti hi mantriṇaḥ.

Vistāritaṃ makara|ketana|dhīvareṇa
strī|saṃjñitaṃ baḍiśam atra bhav'|âmbu|rāśau.
yen' âcirāt tad|adhar'|āmiṣa|lola|martya|
matsyān vikṛṣya vipacaty anurāga|vahnau.

Kāminī|kāya|kāntāre,
kuca|parvata|durgame,
mā saṃcara manaḥ|pāntha,
tatr' âste smara|taskaraḥ.

55 Vyādīrgheṇa calena vakra|gatinā
tejasvinā bhoginā
nīl'|âbja|dyutin" âhinā param ahaṃ
daṣṭo, na tac|cakṣuṣā.
daṣṭe santi cikitsakā diśi diśi,
prāyeṇa dharm'|ârthino.
mugdh'|âkṣ"|īkṣaṇa|vīkṣitasya nahi me
vaidyo na c' âpy auṣadham.

Friend! Retreat
Far from the poisonous fire of her glance,
From her, naturally inconstant,
From that snake called woman, her hood flirtatious gestures.
Bitten by another snake
Herbs can heal a man.
But when he is bitten by that snake who is a clever young woman
Even physicians give up.

The fisherman with the sea monster on his banner has fully extended
His hook—woman—onto the ocean of worldly existence.
Quickly those human fish, lusting for the flesh of her lip,
He hooks. Cooks them in passion's fire.

Into that forest—a sensuous woman's body,
Onto that impassable mountain—her breasts,
Do not wander, wandering mind!
There sits the thief of love!

Once I was bitten by a snake, splendid as the blue lotus,
Curved, virulent, winding,
Sinuous, stretched out,
But not by her eyes.
When I was bitten there were always
Physicians everywhere, seeking a cure.
But if I am beheld in the gaze of a tender-eyed woman,
There is certainly no physician for me, nor any herbal remedy.

Iha hi madhura|gītaṃ, nṛttam etad, raso 'yaṃ,
sphurati parimalo 'sau sparśa eṣa stanānām.
iti hata|param'|ârthair indriyair bhrāmyamāṇaḥ,
svahita|karaṇa|dhūrtaiḥ pañcabhir vañcito 'smi.

Na gamyo mantrāṇāṃ,
    na ca bhavati bhaiṣajya|viṣayo,
na c' âpi pradhvaṃsaṃ
    vrajati vividhaiḥ śāntika|śataiḥ.
bhram'|āveśād aṅge
    kamapi vidadhad|bhaṅgam asakṛt+
smar'|âpasmāro 'yaṃ
    bhramayati dṛśaṃ ghūrṇayati ca.

Jāty|andhāya ca, durmukhāya ca, jarā|
    jīrṇ'|âkhil'|âṅgāya ca,
grāmīṇāya ca, duṣkulāya ca, galat|
    kuṣṭh'|âbhibhūtāya ca
yacchantīṣu manoharaṃ nija|vapur
    lakṣmī|lava|śraddhayā
paṇya|strīṣu, viveka|kalpa|latikā|
    śastriṣu, rajyeta kaḥ.

Veśy" âsau madana|jvālā
    rūp'|êndhana|vivardhitā,
kāmibhir yatra hūyante
    yauvanāni dhanāni ca.

Her sweet voice sparkles,
Her movement shines, her taste thrills,
Her fragrance throbs,
The touch of her breasts excites.
As such, forced to wander about by my senses,
Deprived of their supreme objects,
I am deceived by these five rogues
Who act for their own interest.

It cannot be removed by spells
Nor is it within reach of drugs
Nor destroyed by expiatory rites
In their hundreds.
Like fits—repeatedly causing distress
From the dizziness possessing the body—
Love distorts one's vision,
Turns it upside down.

If—to a man blind from birth, his face ugly,
Entire body wasted by fever,
Vulgar, of bad family,
Overwhelmed by leprosy—
Prostitutes—
Knives to the divine creeper of discrimination—
Give their own enchanting body, hoping for a little
  wealth,
What man will like them?

The courtesan is love's fire,
Strengthened by fuel—her beauty.
Into her, sensuous men sacrifice
Youth and money.

60 Kaś cumbati kula|puruṣo
    veśy"|âdhara|pallavaṃ manojñam api?
cāra|bhaṭa|cora|ceṭaka|
    viṭa|naṭa|niṣṭhīvana|śarāvam.

Dhanyās ta eva, dhaval'|āyata|locanānāṃ
tāruṇya|darpa|ghana|pīna|payodharāṇām
kṣām'|ôdar'|ôpari lasat|trivalī|latānāṃ
dṛṣṭv" ākṛtiṃ, vikṛtim eti mano na yeṣām.

Bāle, līlā|mukulitam amī
    mantharā dṛṣṭi|pātāḥ
kiṃ kṣipyante? virama! virama!
    vyartha eṣa śramas te.
saṃpraty anye vayam, uparataṃ
    bālyam, āsthā vanānte,
kṣīṇo mohas. tṛṇam iva jagaj|
    jālam ālokayāmaḥ.

Iyaṃ bālā māṃ praty
    anavaratam indīvara|dala|
prabhā|coraṃ cakṣuḥ
    kṣipati. kim abhipretam anayā?
gato moho 'smākaṃ!
    smara|śabara|bāṇa|vyatikara|
jvara|jvālā śāntā.
    tad api na varākī viramati.

What man of good family
Kisses the bud-like lip of a courtesan, beautiful though
it might be?
It is a vessel for the spittle of
Spies, warriors, thieves, paramours and actors.

On seeing the shape of women—
Long eyes dazzling bright
Full breasts swollen hard
With youthful pride
Creeper-like folds glistening
Above slender waists—
Those men are fortunate indeed whose
Mind is not perturbed.

Young girl! Why throw those lazy glances,
Your eyes twittering in play?
Stop! Stop!
Your effort is useless.
Now we have changed, our youth has gone,
Our preoccupation is in the forest,
Infatuation destroyed.
We behold this snare-like world almost as grass.

On me ceaselessly this young girl
Casts her eye,
Thief of the blue lotus leaf's splendor.
What does she expect?
My infatuation is gone! The fire from the fever—
Caused by arrows from that wild hunter Love—
Is appeased.
Even then the wretched woman does not cease.

Kiṃ, Kandarpa, śaraṃ kad|arthayasi? re,
kodaṇḍa|ṭaṅkāritam!
re, re, kokila! komalaṃ kala|ravaṃ
kiṃ vā vṛthā jalpasi?
mugdhe, snigdha|vidagdha|cāru|madhurair
lolaiḥ kaṭākṣair alam.
cetaś cumbita|Candracūḍa|caraṇa|
dhyān'|âmṛtaṃ vartate.

65 Virahe 'pi saṃgamaḥ khalu
parasparaṃ saṃgataṃ mano yeṣām.
hṛdayam api vighaṭṭitaṃ cet,
saṅgo virahaṃ viśeṣayati.

«Kiṃ gatena yadi sā na jīvati?
prāṇiti priyatamā tath" âpi kim?»
Ity udīkṣya nava|megha|mālikām
na prayāti pathikaḥ sva|mandiram.

Viramata, budhā, yoṣit|saṅgāt,
sukhāt kṣaṇa|bhaṅgurāt.
kuruta karuṇā|maitrī|prajñā|
vadhū|jana|saṃgamam.
na khalu narake hār'|ākrāntaṃ
ghana|stana|maṇḍalam
śaraṇam, atha vā śroṇī|bimbaṃ
raṇan|maṇi|mekhalam.

Kama, isn't your arrow useless?
Damn the sound of your bow!
Damn! Damn! Cuckoo, why frivolously prattle
Those sweet low notes?
Delicate woman! Enough of your lovely glances,
Sweet, lovely, feigning affection.
My heart lives tasting the ambrosia
Of meditation on moon-crested Shiva's feet.

Even in separation, assuredly stay united 65
The minds of those already mutually united.
If the heart is unlocked
Attachment prefers separation.

"Why go if she does not live?
Why if, however, my beloved breathes?"
This he thought and seeing a garland of fresh clouds
Did not set out for his own home.

Wise men! Cease this pleasurable attachment to women,
Momentary at best.
Associate with the women called
Compassion, friendship, wisdom.
In hell there is certainly no refuge
In irresistible necklaces,
The circle of firm breasts
Or the tinkling jewelled girdle, circling the hip.

Yadā yog'|âbhyāsa|
vyasana|kṛśayor ātma|manasor
avicchinnā maitrī
sphurati kṛtinas, tasya kimu taiḥ?
priyāṇām ālāpair,
adhara|madhubhir, vaktra|vidhubhiḥ,
saniśvās'|āmodaiḥ
sakuca|kalaś'|āśleṣa|surataiḥ?

Yad" āsīd ajñānaṃ
smara|timira|saṃcāra|janitaṃ,
tadā dṛṣṭaṃ nārī|
mayam idam aśeṣaṃ jagad iti.
idānīm asmākaṃ,
paṭutara|vivek'|âñjana|juṣām,
samībhūtā dṛṣṭis
tribhuvanam api Brahma manute.

70 Tāvad eva kṛtinām api sphuraty
eṣa nirmala|viveka|dīpakaḥ,
yāvad eva na kuraṅga|cakṣuṣāṃ
tāḍyate caṭula|locan'|âñcalaiḥ.

Vacasi bhavati saṅga|
tyāgam uddiśya vārtā
śruti|mukhara|mukhānāṃ
kevalaṃ paṇḍitānām.
jaghanam aruṇa|ratna|
granthi|kāñcī|kalāpaṃ
kuvalaya|nayanānāṃ
ko vihātuṃ samarthaḥ?

When—of his mind and self,
Refined by striving after learning and meditation—
Constant friendship sparkles forth,
Does the accomplished man have any use for these?
The chattering of lovely women, lovely lips,
Moon-like faces,
The fragrances of her breathing,
With lovemaking—the embrace of pot-like breasts?

When I was ignorant
By passion's pervading darkness engendered.
Then only of woman appeared to consist
This entire world.
Now I delight in the ointment
Of discrimination most keen,
And my vision has become impartial.
Even the triple-world is Brahma, I conclude.

This clear light of discrimination of the highly skilled
Shines diffusely for just as long as
It is not struck by the tremulous glances
Of the eyes of doe-eyed women.

Talk about
Renunciation of attachment
Occurs only in the speech of learned men,
Mouths eloquent with learning.
But the hip,
Girdled with knots of rubies,
Of lotus-eyed women,
Who truly can forsake it?

Sa para|pratārako 'sau,
nindati yo 'līka|paṇḍito yuvatīḥ.
yasmāt tapaso 'pi phalaṃ
svargaḥ, svarge 'pi c' âpsarasaḥ.

Matt'|êbha|kumbha|dalane bhuvi santi dhīrāḥ,
kecit pracaṇḍa|mṛga|rāja|vadhe 'pi dakṣāḥ,
kiṃtu bravīmi balināṃ purataḥ prasahya,
«Kandarpa|darpa|dalane viralā manuṣyāḥ.»

San|mārge tāvad āste, prabhavati ca naras
tāvad ev' êndriyāṇām,
lajjāṃ tāvad vidhatte, vinayam api samā-
lambate tāvad eva,
bhrū|cāp'|ākṛṣṭa|muktāḥ śravaṇa|patha|gatā
nīla|pakṣmāṇa ete
yāval līlāvatīnāṃ hṛdi na dhṛti|muṣo
dṛṣṭi|bāṇāḥ patanti.

75 Unmatta|prema|saṃrambhād
ārambhante yad aṅganāḥ,
tatra pratyūham ādhātuṃ
Brahm" âpi khalu kātaraḥ.

He just deceives others,
Does every false *pandit* who scorns young girls.
Heaven may be the result of his austerities.
But even in heaven there are nymphs.

In the world some resolute men
Can split the lobes of maddened elephants,
Some are even capable
Of killing enraged lions.
But in front of these powerful men,
I say firmly,
"Few men
Can split Kandárpa's pride."

As long as a man stays on the right path,
As long as he is a master of his senses,
As long as he displays modesty,
As long as he relies on good conduct,
Glances from flirtatious young women,
These arrows destroying resolve—
Reaching to the ears, feathered by eyelashes,
Drawn back, released from the eyebrows, the bow—
Do not penetrate one's heart.

When lovely ladies
Act from impetuosity and frantic love,
Even Brahma is far too frightened
To impede their activity.

Tāvan mahattvaṃ, pāṇḍityaṃ,
kulīnatvaṃ, vivekatā,
yāvaj jvalati n' âṅgeṣu
hataḥ Pañceṣu|pāvakaḥ.

Śāstrajño 'pi, praguṇita|nayo 'py,
ātta|bodho 'pi bāḍham
saṃsāre 'smin bhavati viralo
bhājanaṃ sad|gatīnām.
yen' âitasmin niraya|nagara|
dvāram udghāṭayantī
vām'|âkṣīṇāṃ bhavati kuṭilā
bhrū|latā, kuñcik" êva.

Kṛśaḥ, kāṇaḥ, khañjaḥ, śravaṇa|rahitaḥ, puccha|vikalo,
vraṇī, pūya|klinnaḥ, krimi|kula|śatair āvṛta|tanuḥ,
kṣudhā|kṣāmo, jīrṇaḥ, piṭharaka|kapāl'|ârpita|galaḥ,
śunīm anveti śvā. hatam api ca hanty eva Madanaḥ.

As long as magnanimity, wisdom,
Good family and discrimination are present,
That low Kama
Does not burn my body with his five arrows.

Though he knows the learned texts, though of good
conduct,
Though assuredly enlightened,
It is but a rare man who is a receptacle for the path of the
good
In this transient existence.
Since in it,
There exists the curvaceous arched eyebrows
Of women with delightful eyes,
A key for opening the doors to hell's city.

Emaciated, one-eyed, lame,
Deaf, tail mutilated,
Ulcerated, rotten with pus,
Body covered with swarms of worms,
Wasted from hunger, worn out,
His gullet fixed on a piece of skull.
Thus does a dog follow a bitch.
Love strikes even the wretched.

Strī|mudrāṃ Kusumāyudhasya jayinīṃ,
sarv'|ârtha|sampat|karīṃ
ye mūḍhāḥ pravihāya yānti kudhiyo,
mithyā|phal'|ânveṣiṇaḥ,
te ten' âiva nihatya nirdayataraṃ,
nagnī|kṛtā, muṇḍitāḥ,
kecit pañca|śikhī|kṛtāś ca, jaṭilāḥ
kāpālikāś c' âpare.

80 Viśvāmitra|Parāśara|prabhṛtayo
vāt'|âmbu|parṇ'|âśanās.
te 'pi strī|mukha|paṅka|jaṃ sulalitaṃ
dṛṣṭv" âiva mohaṃ gatāḥ.
śāly|annaṃ saghṛtaṃ payo|dadhi|yutaṃ
ye bhuñjate mānavās,
teṣām indriya|nigraho yadi bhaved,
Vindhyaḥ plavet sāgare.

Parimala|bhṛto vātāḥ, śākhā
nav'|âṅkura|koṭayo,
madhura|vidhur'|ôtkaṇṭhā|bhājaḥ
priyāḥ pika|pakṣiṇām,
virala|virasa|sved'|ôdgārā
vadhū|vadan'|êndavaḥ.
prasarati madhau Dhātryāṃ jāto
na kasya guṇ'|ôdayaḥ.

Madhur ayaṃ madhurair api kokilā|kala|
ravair Malayasya ca vāyubhiḥ
virahiṇaḥ praṇihanti śarīriṇaḥ.
vipadi, hanta, sudh" âpi viṣāyate.

Woman, victorious mark of Kama's weapon,
Brings success in all his goals.
Repudiating her those narrow-minded fools leave,
Searching for false fruits.
Unmercifully assailed by him
To become naked and shaven.
Some are made into five-crest ascetics,
Others have dreadlocks and carry skulls.

Vishva·mitra, Paráshara and the like 80
Eat air, water and leaves.
But when even they see a woman's graceful lotus-like face
They become infatuated.
When men who eat boiled rice
With ghee and coagulated milk
Can restrain their senses,
The Vindhya mountains will float in the sea.

Fragrant breezes,
Branches holding myriad fresh buds,
Cuckoos' wives suffer longingly,
Warbling sweet misery.
Young women,
Moon-like faces barely moist.
As spring proceeds on Earth,
To whom do its superior qualities not appear.

Here is spring,
With its cuckoos sounding sweetly,
Breezes from the Malabar hills,
Destroying lonely men.
Alas, in adversity even ambrosia becomes poison.

Āvāsaḥ kilakiñcitasya, dayitāḥ
pārśve vilās'|âlasāḥ,
karṇe kokila|kāminī|kala|ravaḥ,
smero, latā|maṇṭapaḥ,
goṣṭhī sat|kavibhiḥ samaṃ katipayair,
mugdhāḥ sit'|âṅśoḥ karāḥ,
keṣāṃcit sukhayanti c' âtra hṛdayaṃ
Caitre vicitrāḥ srajaḥ.

Pāntha|strī|virah'|ânal'|āhuti|kalām
ātanvatī mañjarī.
mākandeṣu pik'|âṅganābhir adhunā
sotkaṇṭham ālokyate.
Apy ete nava|pāṭalā|parimala|
prāg|bhāra|pāṭaccarā
vānti klānti|vitāna|tānava|kṛtaḥ Śrī|khaṇḍa|śail'|ânilāḥ?

85 Prathitaḥ: praṇayavatīnāṃ
tāvat padam ātanoti hṛdi mānaḥ,
bhavati na yāvac candana|taru|
surabhir Malaya|pavamānaḥ.

Sahakāra|kusuma|kesara|
nikara|bhar'|āmoda|mūrcchita|dig|ante,
madhura|madhu|vidhura|madhupe
madhau bhavet kasya n' ôtkaṇṭhā?

An abode of sensuous diversion,
Women exhausted by games of allurement nearby,
Sensuous cuckoos murmuring in the ears,
A smile, a bower of creepers.
A meeting with excellent poets,
The moon's delicate rays,
In Spring these colorful garlands
Gladden any man's heart.

Now
A bunch of flowers expresses the offering
To the fire of separation experienced by the traveller's wife.
In the mango trees female cuckoos
Gaze longingly.
Do not these winds from the Malabar mountains,
Stealing the abundant fragrance of fresh trumpet flowers,
Diminish our attenuated weariness?

It is well known: 85
As long as wounded pride
Extends its place in her heart
Of a woman in love
There is no Malabar wind
Fragrant with sandalwood.

Spring.
Horizon pervaded
With the abundant fragrance of mango flowers.
Bees agitated by sweet honey.
Who will not experience longing?

Acch'|âccha|candana|ras'|ārdratarā mṛg'|âkṣyo,
dhārā|gṛhāṇi, kusumāni ca, kaumudī ca,
mando marut, sumanasaḥ, śuci harmya|pṛṣṭhaṃ,
grīṣme madaṃ ca madanaṃ ca vivardhayanti.

Srajo hṛdy'|āmodā,
vyajana|pavanaś, candra|kiraṇāḥ,
parāgaḥ, kāsāro,
malaya|rajaḥ, śīdhu viśadam,
śuciḥ saudh'|ôtsaṅgaḥ,
pratanu vasanaṃ paṅkaja|dṛśo,
nidāgha'|rtāv etad
vilasati labhante sukṛtinaḥ.

Sudhā|śubhraṃ dhāma,
sphurad|amala|raśmiḥ śaśa|dharaḥ,
priyā|vaktr'|âmbhojaṃ,
malayaja|rajaś c' âtisurabhi,
srajo hṛdy'|āmodās,
tad idam akhilaṃ rāgiṇi jane
karoty antaḥ|kṣobhaṃ,
na tu viṣaya|saṃsarga|vimukhe.

90 Taruṇī|veṣ'|ôddīpita|kāmā,
vikasaj|jātī|puṣpa|sugandhiḥ,
unnata|pīna|payodhara|bhārā,
prāvṛṭ tanute kasya na harṣam?

Doe-eyed women,
Bodies moistened,
Bathing rooms,
Flowers and moonlight.
Gentle fragrant breezes,
Splendid roof of a flat mansion,
In summer
Exhilarate lust and passion.

Garlands of enchanting fragrance,
A fanning wind, moon's rays,
Pollen, pools,
Sandalwood powder, clear wine,
Splendid palace roof,
Delicate garment of a lotus-eyed woman.
These, fortunate men obtain
When summer glows.

Whitewashed house,
Moon flawless with flashing rays,
Lovely woman's lotus-face,
Lovely fragrance of sandalwood and dust,
Garlands of enchanting fragrance.
All of this creates turbulence in the sensuous man,
But not in someone
Whose face is turned from the assemblage of senses.

Garment of a young woman desire inflamed,
Fragrance of full-grown jasmine diffusing,
Weight of full breasts uplifted,
The rainy season. Who is not exhilarated?

Viyad upacita|megham̩,
    bhūmayaḥ kandalinyo,
nava|kuṭaja|kadamb'|
    āmodino gandha|vāhāḥ,
śikhi|kula|kala|kekā|
    rāva|ramyā van'|ântāḥ,
sukhinam asukhinam̩ vā
    sarvam utkaṇṭhayanti.

Upari ghanam̩ ghana|paṭalam̩,
    tiryag|girayo 'pi nartita|mayūrāḥ,
kṣitir api kandala|dhavalā.
    dṛṣṭim̩ pathikaḥ kva pātayati?

Ito vidyud|vallī|
    vilasitam, itaḥ ketaki|taroḥ
sphurad|gandhaḥ, prodyaj|
    jalada|ninada|sphūrjitam itaḥ,
itaḥ kekī|krīḍā|
    kalakala|ravaḥ. pakṣmala|dṛśām̩
katham̩ yāsyanty ete
    viraha|divasāḥ sam̩bhṛta|rasāḥ?

Asūci|sam̩cāre,
    tamasi nabhasi prauḍha|jalada|
dhvani|prājñam̩ manye,
    patati pṛṣatānām̩ ca nicaye,
idam̩ saudāmanyāḥ
    kanaka|kamanīyam̩ vilasitam̩
mudam̩ ca mlānim̩ ca
    grathayati pathi svaira|sudṛśām.

Clouds build up in the sky,
Ground clothed with *kándali* flowers,
Wind perfumed with fragrance
Of fresh *kútaja* and *kadámba* trees,
Forests lovely
With troops of peacocks' indistinct cries.
To the happy or wretched man,
It all incites intense longing.

Above—heavy with cloud.
Aside—mountains are dancing peacocks.
Ground—dazzling white.
Where does a traveller cast his glance?

Here flashes of lightning glow,
There quivers the fragrance
Of the *kétaki* tree,
Here a rumbling of heaped up clouds,
There murmurings of peacocks in dalliance.
For women of the long eyelashes,
How will pass these days of separation,
Saturated with love?

When
No path revealed, the sky is dark,
Heavy clouds rumbling whose sound I perceive,
Rain falling in torrents,
Gold-streaked lightning flashes,
Spreading joy and anxiety
On the path for women,
Impulsive and with beautiful eyes.

95 Āsāreṇa na harmyataḥ priyatamair
yātuṃ bahiḥ śakyate.
śīt'|ôtkampa|nimittam āyata|dṛśā
gāḍhaṃ samālingyate.
jātāḥ śīkara|śītalāś ca maruto
raty|anta|sveda|cchido.
dhanyānāṃ bata durdinaṃ sudinatāṃ
yāti priyā|saṃgame.

Ardhaṃ suptvā niśāyāḥ, sarabhasa|surat'|
āyāsa|sanna|ślath'|âṅgaḥ,
prodbhūt'|âsahya|tṛṣṇo, madhu|mada|nirato,
harmya|pṛṣṭhe vivakte,
saṃbhoga|klānta|kāntā|śithila|bhuja|lat"|
āvarjitaṃ karkarīto
jyotsn'|âbhinn'|âccha|dhāraṃ na pibati salilaṃ
śāradaṃ manda|puṇyaḥ.

Hemante dadhi|dugdha|sarpir|aśanā,
mañjiṣṭha|vāso|bhṛtaḥ,
Kāśmīra|drava|sāndra|digdha|vapuṣaś,
chinnā vicitrai rataiḥ,
vṛtt'|ōru|stana|kāminī|jana|kṛt'|
āśleṣā gṛh'|âbhyantare,
tāmbūlī|dala|pūga|pūrita|mukhā
dhanyāḥ sukhaṃ śerate.

Rain—stops her lover 95
Leaving the palace terrace.
Shivering cold—causes a long-eyed woman
To embrace him firmly.
Winds—spring up, bringing cool drizzle,
Removing lovemaking's exudations.
Behold! In meeting a lovely woman,
A bad day is made good for fortunate men.

Having slept half the night,
His body languid, exhausted by impetuous lovemaking,
Raging thirst, drunk on sweet wine,
On a deserted palace roof.
Unfortunate is that man
Who does not drink autumnal water,
Its crystalline streams blended with moonlight,
Poured from a pot
By the trembling slender arm of a woman wearied by love play.

Winter,
Eating ghee and yogurt, wearing bright-red clothes,
Bodies smeared with Kashmiri saffron oil,
Exhausted by splendid plays of love,
Embraced in his house by sensuous women
With round breasts and firm thighs.
Their faces filled with wads of betel nut
Such fortunate men sleep comfortably.

Prodyat|prauḍha|priyaṅgu|dyuti|bhṛti vikasat|
    kunda|mādya|dvirephe
kāle prāleya|vāta|pracala|vilasit'|
    ôdāra|mandāra|dhāmni,
yeṣāṃ no kaṇṭha|lagnā kṣaṇam api tuhina|
    kṣoda|dakṣā mṛg'|âkṣī,
teṣām āyāma|yāmā Yama|sadana|samā
    yāminī yāti yūnām.

Cumbanto gaṇḍa|bhittīr, alakavati mukhe
    sītkṛtāny|ādadhānā,
vakṣaḥs' ûtkañceṣu stana|bhara|pulak'|
    ôdbhedam āpādayantaḥ,
ūrūn ākampayantaḥ pṛthu|jaghana|taṭāt
    sraṃsayanto 'ṅśukāni,
vyaktaṃ kāntā|janānāṃ viṭa|carita|bhṛtaḥ
    śaiśirā vānti vātāḥ.

100 Keśān ākulayan, dṛśo mukulayan,
    vāso balād ākṣipann,
ātanvan pulakodgamaṃ, prakaṭayann
    āvega|kampaṃ śanaiḥ,
vāraṃ vāram udāra|sītkṛtakṛto
    danta|cchadān pīḍayan,
prāyaḥ śaiśira eṣa samprati marut
    kāntāsu kāntāyate.

When the splendor of luxuriant *priyángu* blossoms is magnified,
Huge black bees are intoxicated by the blooming jasmine,
When the house of magnificent *mandára* wood
Shines, shaken by winter winds,
Doe-eyed women, who can remove the cold
By clinging to our necks, even for a moment, are absent.
For men the watch of the night is excessively long,
For the women, night passes as if it were Yama's world.

Kissing the flat cheeks,
Causing gurgles of pleasure on a face with hair pressed flat,
When her chest is uncovered,
Inducing the rising of skin on her breasts.
Shaking her thighs
And loosening the silky folds from the slope of her firm thighs.
Cool winds obviously act like rogues
Toward beautiful women.

Dishevelling her hair, shutting her eyes, 100
Quickly drawing off her clothes,
Thrilling her skin,
Slowly revealing the trepidation of arousal,
Repeatedly squeezing her lips,
Causing lovely gurgling sounds.
This cool wind has become
Mainly like a lover to women.

BHARTRI·HARI: DISENCHANTMENT

C ŪḌ'|ÔTTAṂSITA|candra|cāru|kalikā|
cañcac|chikh"|ābhāsvaraḥ
līlā|dagdha|vilola|Kāma|śalabhaḥ
śreyodaś'|âgre sphuran
antaḥ sphūrjad|apāra|moha|timira|
prāg|bhāram uccāṭayaṃś
cetaḥ sadmani yogināṃ vijayate
jñāna|pradīpo Haraḥ.

Bhrāntaṃ deśam aneka|durga|viṣamaṃ
prāptaṃ na kiṃcit phalam,
tyaktvā jāti|kul'|âbhimānam ucitaṃ
sevā kṛtā niṣphalā,
bhuktaṃ māna|vivarjitaṃ para|gṛheṣv
āśaṅkayā kākavat,
tṛṣṇe! jṛmbhasi pāpa|karma|piśune.
n' âdy' âpi saṃtuṣyasi.

Utkhātaṃ nidhi|śaṅkayā kṣiti|talaṃ,
dhmātā girer dhātavaḥ,
nistīrṇaḥ saritāṃ patir, nṛpatayo
yatnena saṃtoṣitā,ḥ
mantr'|ārādhana|tat|pareṇa manasā
nītāḥ śmaśāne niśāḥ:
prāptaḥ kāṇa|varāṭako 'pi na mayā;
tṛṣṇe, sakāmā bhava.

FROM THE LOVELY CRESCENT moon adorning his head
A tremulous spike of splendid light emerges.
The moth—fickle Kama—he consumed in play,
On the tip of a splendid wick sparkling.
A huge mass of darkness
Of unbounded delusion exploding within, he dispels.
Victorious in the seat of yogins' minds
Is Hara, lamp of knowledge.

Wandered over country rugged and impassable,
Nothing gained.
Gave up the proper pride in family and lineage,
Undertook service with no result.
Empty of pride, ate in others' homes,
Apprehensive like a crow.
Craving! Marker of all evil! You gape.
Even now you are not wholly satisfied.

Suspected treasure, so the ground was dug up,
Minerals from the mountain were smelted,
Ocean crossed,
Kings satisfied diligently.
Nights spent in a cemetery,
Mind entirely engrossed in applying spells.
Not even a cowrie shell I gained.
Craving! Be satisfied.

Khal'|ālāpāḥ soḍhāḥ
katham api tad|ārādhana|paraiḥ,
nigṛhy' ântobāṣpaṃ,
hasitam api śūnyena manasā,
kṛto vitta|stambha|
pratihata|dhiyām añjalir api;
tvam, āśer, mogh'|āśe!
kim aparam ato nartayasi mām?

5 Amīṣāṃ prāṇānāṃ
tulita|bisinī|patra|payasām
kṛte kiṃ n' âsmābhir
vigalita|vivekair vyavasitam?
yad āḍhyānām agre
draviṇa|mada|niḥsaṃjña|manasām
kṛtaṃ māna|vrīḍair
nija|guṇa|kathā|pātakam api.

Kṣāntaṃ na kṣamayā, gṛh'|ôcita|sukhaṃ
tyaktaṃ na saṃtoṣataḥ,
soḍhā duḥsaha|śīta|vāta|tapana|
kleśā, na taptaṃ tapaḥ,
dhyātaṃ vittam ahar|niśaṃ niyamita|
prāṇair na Śambhoḥ padam;
tat tat karma kṛtaṃ yad eva munibhis
tais taiḥ phalair vañcitāḥ.

The taunting ravings of rogues are barely endured
By those bent on appeasing them.
I hold back a suppressed tear,
As if laughing, with heart indifferent.
I even paid homage to those
Stupefied by wealth.
You! Desire! Vain desire!
Why make me dance further?

For the sake of our lives, 5
Mere drops on a lotus leaf,
What would we not do,
Our discernment trickled away?
Since, in the presence of the wealthy,
Senseless minds intoxicated with possessions,
We—in the shame of our conceit,
Wrongly praised our own qualities.

We have been patient, but not from patience,
Have abandoned pleasures of the house, but not with
 satisfaction.
Endured unendurable cold winds and heat,
But have not performed austerities.
Meditated night and day—breath restrained—on
 wealth,
But not on Shánkara's abode.
Sages undertake all this activity,
But we are cheated of every result.

Bhogā na bhuktā vayam eva bhuktāḥ;
tapo na taptaṃ vayam eva taptāḥ;
kālo na yāto vayam eva yātāḥ;
tṛṣṇā na jīrṇā vayam eva jīrṇāḥ.

Valibhir mukham ākrāntaṃ,
paliteṇ' âṅkitaṃ śiraḥ,
gātrāṇi śithilāyante;
tṛṣṇ" âikā taruṇāyate.

Nivṛttā bhog'|êcchā,
puruṣa|bahu|māno 'pi galitaḥ,
samānāḥ svar|yātāḥ
sapadi suhṛdo jīvita|samāḥ,
śanair yaṣṭy|utthānaṃ,
ghana|timira|ruddhe ca nayane;
aho! mūḍhaḥ kāyas
tad api maraṇ'|âpāya|cakitaḥ.

10 Āśā nāma nadī, mano|ratha|jalā,
tṛṣṇā|taraṅg'|ākulā,
rāga|grāhavatī, vitarka|vihagā,
dhairya|druma|dhvaṃsinī,
moh'|āvārta|sudustar'|âtigahanā,
prottuṅga|cintā|taṭī;
tasyāḥ pāra|gatā viśuddha|manaso
nandanti yog'|īśvarāḥ.

I have not experienced sensual pleasures.
I have only experienced.
I did not perform austerities.
I have only suffered.
Time has not elapsed.
I alone have elapsed.
Craving has not deteriorated.
I alone have deteriorated.

My face—overrun with wrinkles,
My head—marked with gray,
My limbs—become flaccid.
Craving alone retains its youth.

Desire for sex has retreated,
What men respect has trickled away,
Esteemed friends, dear as life,
Gone straight to heaven.
Slowly rising with the help of a staff,
Eyes covered by dark clouds.
Damn! Even then the stupid body
Is afraid of disappearing at death.

Desire is this river named, its water—intention, 10
Agitated by—craving as its waves,
Its crocodiles—passion, its birds—imagination.
It destroys the tree—fortitude,
Is impenetrable, its whirlpool—infatuation impossible
to cross,
Its banks—massive anxiety.
Gone beyond her,
Yogic lords of pure minds rejoice.

Na saṃsār'|ôtpannaṃ
    caritam anupaśyāmi kuśalam,
vipākaḥ puṇyānāṃ
    janayati bhayaṃ me vimṛśataḥ,
mahadbhiḥ puṇy'|âughaiś
    cira|parigṛhītāś ca viṣayāḥ
mahānto jāyante
    vyasanam iva dātuṃ viṣayiṇām.

Avaśyaṃ yātāraś ciratаram uṣitv" âpi viṣayāḥ;
viyoge ko bhedas tyajati na jano yat svayam amūn?
vrajantaḥ svātantryād, atula|paritāpāya manasaḥ,
svayaṃ tyaktā hy ete śama|sukham anantaṃ vidadhati.

Brahma|jñāna|viveka|nirmala|dhiyaḥ
    kurvanty aho duṣkaram
yan muñcanty upabhoga|bhāñjy api dhanāni
    ek'|ântato niḥspṛhāḥ;
samprāptān na purā na samprati na ca
    prāptau dṛḍha|pratyayān
vāñchā|mātra|parigrahān api param
    tyaktuṃ na śaktā vayam.

I perceive no auspicious activity
Arisen in this transient existence.
Reflective as I am,
The ripening of my good deeds inspires fear.
By these huge torrents of merit
Sense objects, enjoyed for such a long time,
Grow large and bring disaster
To those attached to the realm of sense desires.

Sense objects stay long in one place,
Yet they move.
What's so special about separation
That a man knowingly abandons them?
Departing of their own volition,
Bringing unequal torment to the mind.
Yet, when abandoned,
Give the endless bliss of tranquility.

Their minds pure from discerning Brahma knowledge.
Amazing! They do what is so difficult,
That though experiencing sense desires,
They give up wealth, utterly without yearning.
There may be no firm confidence
That these have been obtained in the past, nor now, nor in the future,
Yet we are absolutely unable to give up
What is accumulated merely as desire.

Dhanyānāṃ giri|kandareṣu vasatāṃ
jyotiḥ paraṃ dhyāyatām
ānand'|âśru|kaṇān pibanti śakunā
niḥśaṅkam aṅke|śayāḥ;
asmākaṃ tu mano|rath'|ôparacita|prāsāda|vāpī|taṭa|
krīḍā|kānana|keli|kautuka|juṣām
āyuḥ paraṃ kṣiyate.

15 Bhikṣ"|âśanaṃ tad api nīrasam eka|vāram,
śayyā ca bhūḥ, parijano nija|deha|mātram,
vastraṃ viśīrṇa|śata|khaṇḍa|mayī ca kanthā»
hā hā! tath" âpi viṣayā na parityajanti.

Stanau maṅsa|granthī
kanaka|kalaśāv ity upamitau,
mukhaṃ śleṣm'|āgāraṃ
tad api ca śaśāṅkena tulitam,
sravan|mūtra|klinnaṃ
kari|vara|śira|spardhi jaghanam:
muhur nindyaṃ rūpaṃ
kavi|jana|viśeṣair guru kṛtam.

Ekaḥ rāgiṣu rājate priyatamā|
deh'|ârdha|hārī Haraḥ,
nīrāgeṣu jano vimukta|lalan"|
āsaṅgo na yasmāt paraḥ,
durvāra|Smara|bāṇa|pannaga|viṣa|
vyāviddha|mugdho janaḥ
śeṣaḥ kāma|viḍambitān na viṣayān
bhoktuṃ na moktuṃ kṣamaḥ.

Fortunate men dwell in mountain caves,
Meditating on the highest light.
Birds rest on their lap,
Fearlessly drinking their tears of bliss.
But for us—preferring amusements and love-play
In pleasure gardens, on the banks of ponds and in palaces,
Fantasized—
The highest life just withers away.

Tasteless food begged but once a day,
As a bed the ground, company just one's own body,
Clothes, a patchwork of one hundred withered rags.
Damn! Even so, sense objects do not leave.

Her breasts, really just protuberances of flesh
Measured against golden jars.
Her face, just a receptacle of phlegm
Weighed against the moon.
Her thigh, wet with flowing urine,
Rivals the cheek of a majestic elephant.
But look! Her despicable body
Is made highly prized by distinguished poets.

For the passionate, Hara alone shines,
Who carries his wife as half of his body.
For the dispassionate, a person not attracted to sensuous
women has no superior.
The remainder, infatuated
By snakes' venom— Love's irresistible arrows—
Cannot enjoy sense objects, Kama's mockeries,
Nor liberate themselves from them.

Ajānan dāh'|ātmyaṃ
patatu śalabhas tīvra|dahane,
so mīno 'py ajñānād
biḍiśa|yutam aśnātu piśitam,
vijānanto 'py ete
vayam iha vipaj|jāla|jaṭilān
na muñcāmaḥ kāmān:
ahaho! gahano moha|mahimā!

Tṛṣā śuṣyaty āsye
pibati salilaṃ śīta|madhuram,
kṣudh"|ārtaḥ śāly|annaṃ
kavalayati māṅs'|ādi|kalitam,
pradīpte Kām'|âgnau
sudṛḍhataram āliṅgati vadhūm;
pratīkāraṃ vyādheḥ
sukham iti viparyasyati janaḥ.

20 Tuṅgaṃ veśma, sutāḥ satām abhimatāḥ,
saṅkhy"|âtigāḥ saṃpadaḥ,
kalyāṇī dayitā, vayaś ca navam ity
ajñāna|mūḍho janaḥ
matvā viśvam anaśvaraṃ niviśate
saṃsāra|kārā|gṛhe;
saṃdṛśya kṣaṇa|bhaṅguraṃ tad akhilaṃ
dhanyas tu saṃnyasyati.

Ignorant of fire's nature,
A moth inevitably falls into the intense fire.
Similarly the fish,
It must ignorantly eat flesh on the hook.
We too, though, discerning,
Are not released from those
Desires knotting us into misfortune's net.
Alas! Alas! How inpenetrable is infatuation's majesty!

Thirst parches his face,
He drinks water cool and sweet.
Sick with hunger,
He gulps down boiled rice, made palatable as if it were
meat.
Love's fire flares up
And he embraces his wife tightly.
A man is mistaken in thinking
Happiness is the remedy for a problem.

A noble house, sons esteemed by the good,
Prosperity beyond measure,
A lovely wife, the freshness of youth,
A man deluded by ignorance
Considers these as lasting forever,
And enters the prison of transient existence.
But perceiving everything as perishable
The fortunate man gives it up.

Dīnā dīna|mukhaiḥ sad" âiva śiśukair
    ākṛṣṭa|jīrṇ'|âmbarā
krośadbhiḥ kṣudhitair niranna|vidhurā
    dṛśyā na ced gehinī,
yāñcā|bhaṅga|bhayena gadgada|gala|
    truṭyad|vilīn'|âkṣaram
ko «deh' îti» vadet sva|dagdha|jaṭharasy'
    ârthe manasvī pumān?

Abhimata|mahāmāna|granthi|
    prabheda|paṭiyasī,
gurutara|guṇa|grām'|âmbhoja|
    sphuṭ'|ôjjvala|candrikā,
vipula|vilasal|lajjā|vallī|
    vitāna|kuṭhārikā;
jaṭhara|piṭharī duṣpur" êyaṃ
    karoti viḍambanam!

Puṇye grāme vane vā mahati sita|paṭa|
    channa|pāliṃ kapālim
hy ādāya nyāya|garbha|dvija|huta|huta|bhug|
    dhūma|dhūmr'|ôpakaṇṭhe,
dvāraṃ dvāraṃ praviṣṭo varam udara|darī|
    pūraṇāya ksudh"|ārtaḥ
mānī prāṇaiḥ sanātho; na punar anudinaṃ
    tulya|kulyeṣu dīnaḥ.

If it were not for his wife, destitute and starving,
A miserable woman, tattered garments
Pulled at constantly by young children,
Faces miserable, complaining, hungry,
What man of integrity, merely for his own tormented
  belly,
Would say "give,"
The sounds sticking in his throat, breaking into a
  stammer,
Fearful of a rejection of his request?

The highly esteemed knot of pride
It cuts skillfully.
The collection of weighty qualities
Lotus flowers—dimmed by the moon—it is like.
To the expanse of creepers—modesty,
So brightly shining, it is the axe.
Isn't this pot, an insatiable stomach,
A mockery?

That—
Having taken a skull, its edge covered with a white cloth,
Into an auspicious village or a huge forest,
Toward the gray smoke of fire offered by brahmins
According to the Vedas,
He entered every door, sick with hunger,
To fill his cavernous stomach—
Is better for the man of integrity in possession of himself
Than if he goes wretched every day to his kinsmen.

Gaṅgā|taraṅga|kaṇa|śīkara|śītalāni
Vidyādhar'|âdhyuṣita|cāru|śilā|talāni
sthānāni kiṃ Himavataḥ pralayaṃ gatāni
yat s'|âvamāna|para|piṇḍa|ratā manuṣyāḥ?

25 Kiṃ kandāḥ kandarebhyaḥ pralayam upagatā
nirjharā vā giribhyaḥ?
pradhvastā vā tarubhyaḥ sarasa|phala|bhṛto
valkalinyaś ca śākhāḥ?
vīkṣyante yan mukhāni prasabham apagata|
praśrayāṇāṃ khalānām
duḥkh'|āpta|svalpa|vitta|smaya|pavana|vaś'|
ānartita|bhrū|latāni.

Puṇyair mūla|phalais tathā praṇayinīṃ
vṛttiṃ kuruṣv' âdhunā
bhū|śayyāṃ nava|pallavair akṛpaṇair;
uttiṣṭha yāvo vanam,
kṣudrāṇām aviveka|gūḍha|manasāṃ
yatr' ēśvarāṇāṃ sadā
vitta|vyādhi|vikāra|vihvala|girāṃ
nām' âpi na śrūyate.

Cooled by droplets of spray from Ganges' waves
Are the beautiful crags where Vidya·dharas live.
Will such places on Hímavat be destroyed
When men are obsessed with the food of others who
despise them?

Are roots taken from mountain valleys destroyed, 25
And mountain streams?
Are the branches and the bark of trees
—Laden with sap and fruit—destroyed?
That they look to the faces—
Their eyebrows dancing to the air of arrogance about
the minute
Amount of wealth gained with such difficulty—
Of rogues utterly without propriety.

Take up now that happy lifestyle
Of auspicious roots and fruits,
Of fresh clean leaves on the ground for your bed.
Get up, we are going to the forest.
There, not even the name is heard
Of those minuscule Lords,
Minds always confused by lack of discernment,
Voices in agitation, perverted by the disease of wealth.

Phalaṃ sv'|êcchā|labhyaṃ
        prativanam akhedaṃ kṣiti|ruhām,
payaḥ sthāne sthāne
        śiśira|madhuraṃ puṇya|saritām,
mṛdu|sparśā śayyā
        sulalita|latā|pallava|mayī;
sahante saṃtāpaṃ
        tad api dhaninām dvāri kṛpaṇā.

Ye vartante dhana|pati|puraḥ
        prārthanā|duḥkha|bhājaḥ,
ye c' âlpatvaṃ dadhati viṣay'|
        ākṣepa|paryāpta|buddheḥ:
teṣām antaḥ sphurita|hasitaṃ
        vāsarāṇi smareyam,
dhyāna|chede śikhari|kuhara|
        grāva|śayyā|niṣaṇṇaḥ.

Ye saṃtoṣa|nirantara|pramuditās
        teṣāṃ na bhinnā mudo;
ye tv anye dhana|lubdha|saṃkula|dhiyas
        teṣāṃ na tṛṣṇā hatā;
itthaṃ kasya kṛte kṛtaḥ sa Vidhinā
        kīdṛk padaṃ saṃpadam?
svātmany eva samāpta|hema|mahimā,
        Merur na me rocate.

Fruit acquired effortlessly according to choice
From trees in any forest.
Water, cool and sweet,
From auspicious rivers in different places.
A bed, soft to the touch,
Made from young sprouts of caressing creepers.
Even so, these miserable wretches
Put up with pain at the door of the wealthy.

Living in the presence of kings,
They suffer the misery of begging,
Focussing on trivialities,
Because their confused mind is distracted by sense
objects.
I will remember their days,
Laughter exploding in my heart,
At the end of meditation,
Seated on a bed of stones in a mountain cave.

Constantly rejoicing in their satisfaction
They experience no break in their joy.
But others, minds mixed up by lust for wealth,
Never experience the death of craving.
So, for whom did Brahma create Meru,
The epitome of prosperity?
It doesn't please me.
Gold's magnificence is gained only in oneself.

30 Bhikṣ”|āhāram adainyam apratisukhaṃ
bhīti|chidaṃ sarvataḥ
durmātsarya|mad’|âbhimāna|mathanaṃ
duḥkh’|âugha|vidhvaṅsanam,
sarvatr’ ânvaham aprayatna|sulabhaṃ
sādhu|priyaṃ pāvanam,
Śambhoḥ satram avāryam akṣaya|nidhiṃ
śaṅsanti yog’|īśvarāḥ.

Bhoge roga|bhayaṃ, kule cyuti|bhayaṃ,
vitte nṛ|pālād bhayam,
māne dainya|bhayaṃ, bale ripu|bhayaṃ,
rūpe jarāyā bhayam,
śāstre vādi|bhayaṃ, guṇe khala|bhayaṃ,
kāye kṛtāntād bhayam:
sarvaṃ vastu bhay’|ânvitaṃ Bhuvi nṛṇāṃ,
vairāgyam ev’ âbhayam.

Ākrāntaṃ maraṇena janma, jarasā
c’ âtyujjvalaṃ yauvanam,
saṃtoṣo dhana|lipsayā, śama|sukhaṃ
prauḍh’|âṅganā|vibhramaiḥ,
lokair matsaribhir guṇā, vana|bhuvo
vyālair, nṛpā durjanaiḥ,
asthairyeṇa vibhūtayo ’py upahatā:
grastaṃ na kiṃ kena vā?

Begged food, a salubrious condition,
Great happiness, absence of fear toward anything,
Destruction of conceit, arrogance and malicious envy,
Shattering the torrent of misery.
Everywhere, every day it is gained effortlessly,
It is loved by the good and pure.
Lordly yogins praise this imperishable treasure of Shiva,
Satisfying, irresistible.

In pleasure there is fear of disease, in a family fear of disgrace,
In wealth fear of the king,
In pride fear of wretchedness, in an army fear of the enemy,
In beauty fear of decay,
In *shastric* knowledge fear of sophistry, in a man of good quality fear of a rogue,
In the body fear of death.
Every situation contains fear for men on Earth,
Alone the state of dispassion has no fear.

Birth is defeated by death,
Youth's absolute splendor by old age,
Satisfaction by lust for wealth,
Restful happiness by audacious women's flirtatious gestures,
Men of good quality by selfish people,
Forests by wild elephants, kings by bad men.
Even prosperity is corrupted by instability.
What is not swallowed up by something?

Ādhi|vyādhi|śatair janasya vividhair
ārogyam unmūlyate,
lakṣmīr yatra patanti tatra vivṛta|
dvārā iva vyāpadaḥ,
jātaṃ jātam avaśyam āśu vivaśaṃ
mṛtyuḥ karoty ātmasāt:
tat kiṃ tena niraṅkuśena vidhinā
yan nirmitaṃ susthiram?

Bhogās tuṅga|taraṅga|bhaṅga|taralāḥ,
prāṇāḥ kṣaṇa|dhvaṅsinaḥ,
stokāny eva dināni yauvana|sukha|
sphūrtiḥ priyāsu sthitā:
tat saṃsāram asāram eva nikhilaṃ
buddhvā budhā bodhakāḥ
lok'|ânugraha|peśalena manasā
yatnaḥ samādhīyatām.

35 Bhogā megha|vitāna|madhya|vilasat|
saudāminī|cañcalāḥ,
āyur vāyu|vighaṭṭit'|âbja|paṭalī|
līn'|âmbuvad|bhaṅguram,
lolā yauvana|lālasās tanubhṛtām:
ity ākalayya drutam
yoge dhairya|samādhi|siddhi|sulabhe
buddhiṃ vidadhvaṃ budhāḥ.

By hundreds of varieties of physical and mental pain
A man's good health is eradicated.
Prosperity may be in him,
But disasters fall on him like open doors.
Birth after birth, quickly, certainly,
Death makes your self his own.
Is anything made secure
By unchecked fate?

Tottering pleasures crash like huge waves,
Living beings can be destroyed in an instant,
Youth's bursting forth into happiness
Stays in beautiful woman but for a few days.
Knowing this entire transient existence has no substance,
Wise teachers
Concentrate diligently
With a mind skilled in helping people.

For humans sense pleasures flicker 35
Like lightning flashing amid the canopy of cloud,
Life is fragile as water clinging
To the edge of the wind-buffeted lotus.
Fickle are the yearnings of youth.
Reflect on this right now,
And fix your mind in meditation,
Easy to achieve by those perfected in concentration and resolve.

Āyuḥ kallola|lolaṃ, katipaya|divasa|
 sthāyinī yauvana|śrīḥ,
s'|ârthāḥ saṃkalpa|kalpā, ghana|samaya|taḍid|
 vibhramā bhoga|pūgāḥ,
kaṇṭh'|āśleṣ'|ôpagūḍhaṃ tad api ca na ciraṃ
 yat priyābhiḥ praṇītam;
Brahmaṇy āsakta|cittā bhavata bhava|bhay'|
 âmbhodhi|pāraṃ tarītum.

Kṛcchreṇ' âmedhya|madhye niyamita|tanubhiḥ
 sthīyate garbha|vāse,
kāntā|viśleṣa|duḥkha|vyatikara|viṣamo
 yauvane c' ôpabhogaḥ,
vām'|âkṣīnām avajñā|vihasita|vasatir
 vṛddha|bhāvo 'py asādhuḥ;
saṃsāre, re manuṣyā, vadata yadi sukhaṃ
 svalpam apy asti kiṃcit.

Vyāghr" îva tiṣṭhati jarā paritarjayantī,
rogāś ca śatrava iva praharanti deham,
āyuḥ parisravati bhinna|ghaṭād iv' âmbhaḥ,
lokas tath" âpy ahitam ācarat' îti citram.

Life is a wave-like movement.
Youth's beauty lasts only a few days.
Wealth is like a momentary thought.
Multifarious enjoyments flash as lightning in the rainy season.
A hidden embrace on the neck
Contrived by lovely women,
Even that too does not last.
Attach your minds to Brahma
To cross the fearful ocean of existence.

In the womb it exists in pain,
Limbs contracted in the midst of piss and shit.
Enjoyment in youth is variable,
Mixed with misery following separation from one's beloved.
Even venerable old age is unsatisfactory.
One dwells in the laughter and derision of lovely-eyed women.
Hey! Men, speak up,
If there is even the slightest happiness in transient existence.

Like a tiger old age is thoroughly menacing,
And like enemies diseases ravage the body.
Like water from a broken pot life flows away.
Even so, it is amazing how people act unfavorably to themselves.

Bhogā bhaṅgura|vṛttayo bahu|vidhās
tair eva c' âyaṃ bhavaḥ,
tat kasy' êha kṛte paribhramata, re
lokāḥ? kṛtaṃ ceṣṭitaiḥ,
āśā|pāśa|śat'|ôpaśānti|viśadaṃ
cetaḥ samādhīyatām
kām'|ôtpatti|vaśāt sva|dhāmani yadi
śraddheyam asmad|vacaḥ.

40 Brahm"|êndr'|ādi|marud|gaṇān tṛṇa|kaṇān
yatra sthito manyate,
yat svādād virasā bhavanti vibhavas
trailokya|rājy'|ādayaḥ,
bhogaḥ ko 'pi sa eka eva paramo
nity'|ôdito jṛmbhate;
bho sādho! kṣaṇa|bhaṅgure tad|itare
bhoge ratiṃ mā kṛthāḥ.

Sā ramyā nagarī, mahāt sa nṛpatiḥ,
sāmanta|cakraṃ ca tat
pārśve, tasya ca sā vidagdha|pariṣat,
tāś candra|bimb'|ânanāḥ,
udvṛttaḥ sa ca rāja|putra|nivahas,
te bandinas, tāḥ kathāḥ;
sarvaṃ yasya vaśād agāt smṛti|pathaṃ
Kālāya tasmai namaḥ.

Sense enjoyments are multifarious transient events,
Of which existence is formed.
Why do men wander about in it?
Hey! Enough of activities.
If our words are to be trusted,
Focus onto your own heart your mind,
Now purified from the power of compulsive desire
By the cessation of those many hopes which are bonds.

When he considers the hosts of deities led by Indra, 40
and Brahma
To be a snippet of grass,
The taste of That* renders sour powers like sovereignty of
the triple-world.
One particular sense enjoyment alone is unique and
supreme,
Arises continually and unfolds.
Hey! Good man! In this state of transitoriness,
Take no delight in any other sense object.

His city is lovely, he is a great king,
His circle of allies stays near him,
His assembly is of shrewd men,
His women's face like the moon's disc.
He is proud, has many sons,
Panegyrists and tales of praise.
Obeisance to him, Time,
Under whose power everything has receded into memory.

Yatr' ânekaḥ kvacid api gṛhe,
tatra tiṣṭhaty ath' âikaḥ,
yatr' âpy ekas tad anu bahavas,
tatra n' âiko 'pi c' ânte;
itthaṃ neyau rajani|divasau
lolayad dvāv iv' âkṣau
Kālaḥ kalyo bhuvana|phalake
krīḍati prāṇi|śāraiḥ.

Ādityasya gat'|āgatair ahar|ahaḥ
saṃkṣīyate jīvitam;
vyāpārair bahu|kārya|bhāra|gurubhiḥ
kālo 'pi na jñāyate;
dṛṣṭvā janma|jarā|vipatti|maraṇaṃ
trāsaś ca n' ôtpadyate;
pītvā moha|mayīṃ pramāda|madirām
unmatta|bhūtaṃ jagat.

«Rātriḥ s" âiva punaḥ sa eva divaso»
matvā mudhā jantavaḥ
dhāvanty udyaminas tath"| âiva nibhṛta|
prārabdha|tat|tat|kriyāḥ
vyāpāraiḥ punar ukta|bhūta|viṣayair:
itthaṃ vidhen' âmunā
saṃsāreṇa kad|arthitā vayam aho
mohān na lajjāmahe.

ometimes many are in the house,
Then just one.
Even when just one, many come after that.
Finally there is not even one.
Like this are day and night guided,
Clever Time setting them in motion like two dice,
Playing with living beings as the pieces,
On the earth as gaming board.

With the daily coming and going of the sun,
Life declines.
With the heavy burden of life's daily obligatory duties,
Even time is not perceived.
At the sight of birth, old age, disaster and death,
Fear is not provoked.
On drinking the intoxicating liquor of infatuation,
The world becomes mad.

"It is simply night and simply day again."
Musing on this people uselessly
Pursue the accomplishment of every action,
Undertaken in private,
Striving due to habitual activities, their pleasures
experienced before.
In this way transient existence
Has made us useless,
But, infatuated, we are not ashamed.

45 Na dhyātaṃ padam Īśvarasya vidhivat
saṃsāra|vicchittaye;
svarga|dvāra|kavāṭa|pāṭana|paṭur
Dharmo 'pi n' ôpārjitaḥ;
nārī|pīna|payodhar'|ōru|yugalaṃ
svapne 'pi n' āliṅgitam;
mātuḥ kevalam eva yauvana|vana|
chede kuṭhārā vayam.

N' âbhyastā prativādi|vṛnda|damanī
vidyā vinīt'|ôcitā,
khaḍg'|âgraiḥ kari|kumbha|pīṭha|dalanair
nākaṃ na nītaṃ yaśas,
kāntā|komala|pallav'|âdhara|rasaḥ
pīto na candr'|ôdaye;
tāruṇyaṃ gatam eva niṣphalam aho
śūny'|ālaye dīpavat!

Vidyā n' âdhigatā kalaṅka|rahitā, vittaṃ ca n' ôpārjitam,
śuśruṣ" âpi samāhitena manasā pitror na saṃpāditā,
ālol'|āyāta|locanāḥ priyatamāḥ svapne 'pi n' āliṅgitāḥ;
Kālo 'yaṃ para|piṇḍa|lolupatayā kākair iva preryate.

We did not meditate properly on Shiva's foot 45
To cut asunder transient existence.
We did not cultivate the Law
For bringing down the door of heaven.
Even in a dream we did not embrace
A woman's pair of thighs or her full breasts.
We are simply axes
For cutting the forest called youth—of the mother.

Knowledge—for subduing hosts of rivals and fit for the
cultivated,
Was not learned.
Fame—acquired by tearing elephants' frontal lobes with
sharp swords,
Did not lead to heaven.
The taste—of a young girl's tender fresh lips,
Was not drunk at moonrise.
Beware! Youth has gone utterly, fruitless.
Like a light in an empty house.

Knowledge was not acquired flawlessly,
Nor wealth gained,
Obedience toward parents was not practiced
With composed mind,
Young girls, long eyes trembling,
Not embraced even in a dream.
Time is urged along
As if by crows greedy for others' food.

Vayaṃ yebhyo jātāś
cira|paricitā eva khalu te,
samaṃ yaiḥ saṃvṛddhāḥ
smṛti|viṣayatāṃ te 'pi gamitāḥ;
idānīm ete smāḥ
pratidivasam āsanna|patanāḥ
gatās tuly'|âvasthāṃ
sikatila|nadī|tīra|tarubhiḥ.

Āyur varṣa|śataṃ nṛṇāṃ parimitaṃ
rātrau tad ardhaṃ gatam,
tasy' ârdhasya parasya c' ârdham aparaṃ
bālatva|vṛddhatvayoḥ,
teṣāṃ vyādhi|viyoga|duḥkha|sahitaṃ
sev"|ādibhir nīyate;
jīve vārita|raṅga|cañcalatare
saukhyaṃ kutaḥ prāṇinām?

50 Kṣaṇaṃ bālo bhūtvā, kṣaṇam api yuvā kāma|rasikaḥ,
kṣaṇaṃ vittair hīnaḥ, kṣaṇam api ca saṃpūrṇa|vibhavaḥ,
jarā|jīrṇair aṅgair naṭa iva valī|maṇḍita|tanuḥ,
naraḥ saṃsār'|ânte viśati Yama|dhānī|yavanikām.

We were born from them
Who became long familiar.
We grew up with them
Who have been sent to the land of memory.
Now, each day,
We are approaching death,
Arrived at the same condition
As trees on a sandy riverbank.

A man's life is one hundred years.
Half is gone with sleep in the night.
Of the other half, another half is
Taken up with old age and youth.
For living beings it is spent in servitude and the like,
Bringing with it pain, separation and sickness.
In this so unsteady wave-like life,
How can there be happiness for them?

For a moment a child,
For a moment also a youth savoring the sensuous,
For a moment poor,
For a moment flush with wealth.
But when his limbs are withered, body adorned with
wrinkles,
He is like an actor.
At the end of this transient existence
That man enters the veil of Yama's world.

Tvaṃ rājā, vayam apy upāsita|guru|
prajñ"|âbhimān'|ônnatāḥ;
khyātas tvaṃ vibhavair, yaśāṃsi kavayo
dikṣu pratanvanti naḥ:
itthaṃ māna|dhan'|âtidūram ubhayor
apy avayor antaram;
yady asmāsu parāṅmukho 'si, vayam apy
ekāntato niḥspṛhāḥ.

Arthānām īśiṣe tvaṃ, vayam api ca girām
īśmahe yāvad artham;
śūras tvaṃ, vādi|darpa|vyupaśamana|vidhāv
akṣayaṃ pāṭavaṃ naḥ;
sevante tvāṃ dhan'|āḍhyā, mati|mala|hataye
mām api śrotu|kāmāḥ;
mayy apy āsthā na te cet, tvayi mama nitarām
eva Rājann an|āsthā.

Vayam iha parituṣṭā valkalais, tvaṃ dukūlaiḥ;
sama iva paritoṣo, nirviśeṣo viśeṣaḥ;
sa tu bhavatu daridro yasya tṛṣṇā viśālā:
manasi ca parituṣṭe ko 'rthavāt, ko daridraḥ?

You are king.
We also are pridefully uplifted in the wisdom of respected teachers.
You are famous by your majesty.
poets extend our renown everywhere.
Just so, between both of us
There is no great distance in riches and honor.
If you are hostile to us
We are utterly unconcerned.

You have wealth
And I too have words—its equivalent.
You are a hero.
Extinction of the feverish pride of eloquence is my undying skill.
Wealthy people who serve you
Want also to hear me for removing blemishes in the mind.
If you have no respect for me
I have absolutely no respect for you, King.

We are happy with bark garments
And you with fine cloth.
Satisfaction is virtually the same,
Any difference is no difference.
But anyone beset by enormous craving
Will be a pauper.
When the mind is entirely happy
Who is wealthy, who is poor?

Phalam alam aśanāya,
 svādu pānāya toyam,
kṣitir api śayan'|ârthaṃ,
 vāsase valkalaṃ ca;
nava|dhana|madhu|pāna|
 bhrānta|sarv'|êndriyāṇām
avinayam anumantuṃ
 n' ôtsahe durjānām.

55 Aśīmahi vayaṃ bhikṣām,
 āśā|vāso vasīmahi,
śayīmahi mahī|pṛṣṭhe:
 kurvīmahi kim īśvaraiḥ?

Na naṭā, na viṭā, na gāyakāḥ,
na ca sabhy'|êtara|vāda|cañcavaḥ,
nṛpam īkśitum atra ke vayam?
stana|bhār'|ānamitā na yoṣitaḥ.

Vipula|hṛdayair īśair etaj
 janitaṃ purā;
vidhṛtam aparair dattaṃ c' ânyair
 vijitya tṛṇaṃ yathā;
iha hi bhuvanāny anye dhīrāś
 catur|daśa bhuñjate;
katipaya|pura|svāmye puṃsāṃ
 ka eṣo mada|jvaraḥ?

Fruit is enough for food,
Sweet water for drinking,
The mere ground serves for a bed,
And bark clothes.
Of those wicked people, whose total senses have
wandered
After sipping the nectar of trifling wealth
I cannot approve
The misconduct.

We can eat begged food, 55
We can go naked,
We can sleep on the ground.
What need have we of kings?

Not actors, nor flatterers, nor singers,
Nor famous for vulgar speech are we.
Do we want to see the king?
Nor are we women bowed down by ample breasts.

Long ago was this world produced
By gods of expansive hearts.
Some kings protected it,
Others conquered and gave it away like grass.
Even now other resolute men
Enjoy the fourteen worlds.
What is this fever of arrogance
In men, lords over just a few towns?

Abhuktāyāṃ yasyāṃ
kṣaṇam api na jātaṃ nṛpa|śataiḥ
Bhuvas tasyā lābhe
ka iva bahumānaḥ kṣiti|bhṛtām?
tad|aṃśasy' âpy aṃśe
tad|avayava|leśe 'pi patayaḥ
viṣāde kartavye,
vidadhati jaḍāḥ pratyuta mudam.

Mṛt|piṇḍo jala|rekhayā valayitaḥ sarvo
apy ayaṃ nanv aṇuḥ,
sv'|âṃśī|kṛtya tam eva saṃgara|śatai
rājñāṃ gaṇā bhuñjate;
te dadyur dadato 'thavā kim aparaṃ
kṣudrā daridrā bhṛśam;
dhig! dhik! tān puruṣ'|âdhamān dhana|kaṇān
vañchanti tebhyo 'pi ye.

60 Sa jātaḥ ko 'py āsīn,
Madana|ripuṇā mūrdhni dhavalam
kapālaṃ yasy' ôccair
vinihitam alaṃkāra|vidhaye;
nṛbhiḥ prāṇa|trāṇa|
pravaṇa|matibhiḥ kaiś cid adhunā
namadbhiḥ kaḥ puṃsām
ayam atula|darpa|jvara|bharaḥ?

There has not been even a moment
When the Earth has not been enjoyed by hundreds of kings.
What is the king's massive pride
In gaining the Earth?
When they should be depressed
About a portion
Or even a minute portion of her,
Stupid kings experience joy instead.

A lump of earth enclosed by the ocean.
No matter how small in its entirety,
Hosts of kings enjoy it
Once they have taken their own portion with hundreds of soldiers.
They should give or they do give.
How difficult is it for the other poverty-stricken kings.
Damn! Damn! Those low men of minuscule wealth
Who want things from them.

A certain man was born, 60
His splendid skull
Placed by Shiva
On his own head as an ornament.
Why do men experience
An excessive fever of unequalled pride
Because some men
Who think only of preserving their own life bow to them?

Pareṣāṃ cetāṃsi
        pratidivasam ārādhya bahudhā,
prasādaṃ kiṃ netuṃ
        viśasi, hṛdaya, kleśa|kalitam?
prasanne tvayy antaḥ
        svayam udita|cintā|maṇi|gaṇaḥ.
viviktaḥ saṃkalpaḥ
        kim abhilaṣitaṃ puṣyati na te?

Paribhramasi kiṃ mudhā?
        kva|cana, citta, viśrāmyatāṃ!
svayaṃ bhavati yad yathā,
        bhavati tat tathā n' ânyathā;
atītam an|anusmarann
        api ca bhāvya|saṃkalpayann,
atarkita|samāgamān
        anubhavāmi bhogān aham.

Etasmād viram' êndriy'|ârtha|gahanād
        āyāsakād, āśraya
śreyo|mārgam aśeṣa|duḥkha|śamana|
        vyāpāra|pakṣaṃ kṣaṇāt;
svātmī|bhāvam upaihi, saṃtyaja nijāṃ
        kallola|lolāṃ gatim;
mā bhūyo bhaja bhaṅgurāṃ bhava|ratiṃ,
        cetaḥ, prasīd' âdhunā!

Every day after various propitiations
To the hearts of others,
Why, heart, are you entering what gives so much pain,
Just to curry favors?
When you are pleased within,
Hosts of wish-granting gems* appear effortlessly.
Your desire being pure,
What desire will not nourish you?

Why do you wander about aimlessly?
Mind, rest somewhere!
What is is by itself.
So it will be, and not otherwise.
Even though not worrying about the past,
Nor anticipating the future,
I will not enjoy sense pleasures,
Whose arrival is unexpected.

Draw back from that inpenetrable object of the senses,
It is most wearisome.
Follow the path of bliss,
Capable instantly of suppressing all troubles.
Find your own true self,
Abandon completely your inherent path, unstable as a
wave.
Cultivate no longer worldly existence's transient path.
Mind, stay clear!

Moham mārjaya! tām upārjaya ratiṃ
candr'|ârdha|cūḍā|maṇau!
cetaḥ! svarga|taraṅgiṇī|taṭa|bhuvām
āsaṅgam aṅgī|kuru;
ko vā vīciṣu, budbudeṣu ca, taḍil|
lekhāsu ca, strīṣu ca
jvāl'|âgreṣu ca, pannageṣu ca, suhṛd|
vargeṣu ca pratyayaḥ?

65 Cetaś! cintaya mā ramāṃ sakṛd imām
asthāyinīm āsthāya
bhū|pāla|bhru|kuṭī|kuṭī|viharaṇa|
vyāpāra|paṇy'|âṅganām;
kanthā|kañcukinaḥ praviśya bhavana|
dvārāṇi Vārāṇasī|
rathyā|paṅktiṣu pāṇi|pātra|patitāṃ
bhikṣām apekṣāmahe.

Agre gītaṃ, sarasa|kavayaḥ
pārśvayor Dākṣiṇātyāḥ,
paścād līlā|valaya|raṇitaṃ
cāmara|grāhiṇīnām;
yady asty evaṃ kuru bhava|ras'|
āsvādane lampaṭatvam,
no cec cetaḥ! praviśa sahasā
nirvikalpe samādhau.

Prāptaḥ śriyaḥ sakala|kāma|dughās, tataḥ kiṃ?
nyastaṃ padaṃ śirasi vidviṣatāṃ, tataḥ kim?
saṃpāditāḥ praṇayino vibhavais, tataḥ kiṃ?
kalpa|sthitās tanu|bhṛtāṃ tanavas, tataḥ kim?

Wipe away infatuation!
Focus on the crest-jewel of the moon!
Mind! Affirm attachment
To the bank of the heavenly Ganges.
Is there confidence in waves, bubbles,
Flashes of lightning and women,
Tips of flames, snakes
And one's collection of friends?

Mind! Right now do not focus anxiously on 65
This lovely courtesan
Whose occupation is dwelling in a hut
According to the king's whim.
Wearing rags,
We enter doors in the streets of Varánasi,
Hoping for food
Fallen onto the hand with which we drink.

In front song,
On both sides sophisticated poets from the South,
Behind, the ringing sound of splendid armlets
Of female chowrie-bearers.
If this is it,
Cultivate a lust for the taste of worldly existence.
If not,
Mind! Immediately enter pure concentration.

Riches were gained giving every desire. Then what?
Foot placed on your enemy's head. Then what?
Friends acquired because of wealth. Then what?
Human bodies lasting an aeon. Then what?

Bhaktir Bhave, maraṇa|janma|bhayaṃ hṛdi|stham,
sneho na bandhuṣu, na manmatha|jā vikārāḥ,
saṃsarga|doṣa|rahitā vijanā vanāntāḥ:
vairāgyam asti; kim itaḥ param arthanīyam?

Tasmād anantam ajaraṃ paramaṃ vikāsi
tad Brahma cintaya! kim ebhir asad|vikalpaiḥ?
yasy' ânuṣaṅgina ime bhuvan'|ādhipatya|
bhog'|ādayaḥ kṛpaṇa|loka|matā bhavanti.

70 Pātālam āviśasi, yāsi nabho vilaṅghya,
diṅ|maṇḍalaṃ bhramasi mānasaś cāpalena;
bhrānty" âpi jātu vimalaṃ katham ātmanīnam
na Brahma saṃsmarasi nirvṛtim eṣi yena?

Devotion to Shiva,
Fear of death and birth in one's heart,
No affection toward kinsmen,
No emotions born from love,
Isolated woods,
Devoid of the flaws of association with men.
This is dispassion.
What more could be asked?

Therefore, on that eternal, undecaying, supreme,
all-pervading
Brahma, focus! What's the use of evil ambitions?
From association with That* follows sovereignty
And other pleasures esteemed by miserable people.

Mind! You enter the underworld, 70
Go beyond heaven,
Wander the horizon,
With your fickle nature.
Even though you are confused,
Why do you never remember
That stainless Brahma, auspicious for yourself,
By whom you will achieve repose?

Kiṃ Vedaiḥ, smṛtibhiḥ, Purāṇa|paṭhanaiḥ,
śāstrair mahā|vistaraiḥ?
svarga|grāma|kuṭī|nivāsa|phala|daiḥ
karma|kriyā|vibhramaiḥ?
muktv" âikaṃ bhava|duḥkha|bhāra|racanā|
vidhvaṅsa|kāl'|ânalam
sv'|ātm'|ānanda|pada|praveśa|kalanaṃ,
śeṣair vaṇig|vṛttibhiḥ.

Yato Meruḥ śrīmān
nipatati yug'|ânt'|âgni|valitaḥ,
samudrāḥ śuṣyanti
pracura|makara|grāha|nilayāḥ,
Dharā gacchaty antaṃ
dharaṇi|dhara|pādair api dhṛtā,
śarīre kā vārtā
kari|kalabha|karṇ'|âgra|capale?

Gātraṃ saṃkucitaṃ, gatir vigalitā,
bhraṣṭā ca dant'|āvaliḥ;
dṛṣṭir naśyati, vardhate badhiratā,
vaktraṃ ca lālāyate;
vākyaṃ n' ādriyate ca, bāndhava|jano
bhāryā na śuśrūṣate:
hā kaṣṭaṃ! puruṣasya jīrṇa|vayasaḥ
putro 'py amitrāyate.

What use are the Vedas, the traditional texts,
Reciting the *Purána*s, and the learned treatises, utterly copious?
And the flurry of activity involved in religious rituals
Giving as a result heaven, which is like dwelling in a village hut?
Except for that alone which produces entry into the blissful abode of one's self,
Which is like the destructive fire destroying
The anguish-filled accoutrements—the burden of miserable existence;
All else is just the posturings of merchants.

Since illustrious Meru,
Circled by fire at the cosmic period's end, falls.
Since the ocean,
Home to multitude sea monsters and large fish, dries up.
Since the Earth,
Supported even by the feet of huge mountains, is destroyed.
What to say of the body,
Unsteady as the tip of a young elephant's ear?

His body wizened up, his step slipped away,
Teeth broken,
Vision destroyed, deafness grows,
Mouth dribbles,
His command not respected, neither kinsmen
Nor wife obedient.
How painful! Even the son of a man of decayed age
Becomes his enemy.

Varṇaṃ sitaṃ jhaṭiti vīkṣya śiro|ruhāṇām
sthānaṃ jarā|paribhavasya tadā pumāṅsam,
āropit'|âsthi|śatakaṃ parihṛtya, yānti
caṇḍāla|kūpam iva dūrataraṃ taruṇyaḥ.

75 Yāvat svastham idaṃ śarīram arujaṃ,
yāvaj jarā dūrato,
yāvac c' êndriya|śaktir aprati|hatā,
yāvat kṣayo n' āyuṣaḥ,
ātma|śreyasi tāvad eva viduṣā
kāryaḥ prayatno mahān
saṃdīpte bhavane tu kūpa|khananaṃ
pratyudyamaḥ kīdṛśaḥ?

Tapasyantaḥ santaḥ kim adhinivasāmaḥ sura|nadīm?
guṇ'|ôdārān dārān uta paricarāmaḥ sa|vinayam?
pibāmaḥ śāstr'|âughān uta vividha|kāvy'|âmṛta|rasān?
na vidmaḥ kiṃ kurmaḥ katipaya|nimeṣ'|āyuṣi jane!

Durārādhyāś c' âmī
turaga|cala|cittāḥ kṣiti|bhujaḥ,
vayaṃ ca sthūl'|êcchāḥ
sumahati phale baddha|manasaḥ,
jarā dehaṃ mṛtyur
harati dayitaṃ jīvitam idam;
sakhe! n' ânyac chreyo
jagati viduṣo 'nyatra tapasaḥ.

Immediately,
On seeing the white of his hair,
Then the state of a man humiliated by old age,
Shunning him as a hundred cast-away bones,
Young women flee far away, as if he were the cave of an outcaste.

While the body is sound, without disease, 75
While old age is distant,
While the power of the senses is unhindered,
While there is no decline in life-force,
Even up to the bliss of the self
Should a wise man make a huge effort,
For when one's house has burned
What is the point of striving to build a hole?

Shall we dwell on the heavenly river,
Performing austerities?
Or shall we modestly court women with lovely qualities?
Or shall we imbibe the torrents of learned treatises
Redolent with the immortal sentiments of many poems?
We don't know what to do
In life that is just a blink!

Difficult to please are
Kings' minds, which move like horses.
But we want wealth,
Out minds are set on a massive result.
Old age takes our body,
Death our beloved life.
Friend! For a wise man there is no wealth in this world
Except for austerities.

Māne mlāyini, khaṇḍite ca vasuni,
vyarthe prayāte 'rthini,
kṣīṇe bandhu|jane, gate parijane,
naṣṭe śanair yauvane,
yuktaṃ kevalam etad eva sudhiyāṃ:
yaj Jahnu|kany"|âpayaḥ
pūta|grāva|gir'|îndra|kandara|naṭī|
kuñje nivāsaḥ kva cit.

Ramyāś candra|marīcayas, tṛṇavatī
ramyā van'|ântaḥ|sthalī,
ramyaṃ sādhu|samāgam'|āgata|sukhaṃ,
kāvyeṣu ramyāḥ kathāḥ,
kop'|ôpāhita|bāṣpa|bindu|taralaṃ
ramyaṃ priyāyā mukham;
sarvaṃ ramyam anityatām upagate
citte na kiṃ cit punar.

80 Ramyaṃ harmya|talaṃ na kiṃ vasataye
śrāvyaṃ na gey'|ādikam?
kiṃ vā prāṇa|samā|samāgama|sukhaṃ
n' âiv' âdhika|prītaye?
kiṃ tu bhrānta|pataṅga|pakṣa|pavana|
vyālola|dīp'|âṅkurac|chāyā|
cañcalam ākalayya, sakalaṃ
santo vanāntaṃ gatāḥ.

When pride weakens, wealth fragments,
A request is unrealized,
Relatives decrease, retinue gone,
And youth gradually vanished.
One thing alone is suitable for the wise:
A dwelling in a hut of creepers,
On gravel purified by Ganges' water,
Somewhere in the valley of a huge mountain.

Lovely are the moon's rays,
Lovely the grass-filled forest clearing,
Lovely the happiness produced by a meeting of good
  people,
Lovely the tales in poems,
Lovely is a woman's face
Trembling with angry teardrops.
Nothing is lovely again
When the mind rests on what is transient.

Isn't a palace roof lovely for a dwelling, 80
Songs and the like lovely to hear?
Or isn't happiness in meeting with a woman
Conducive to great joy?
However, when they examined
The moving splendor of a lamp's flame
Swaying with the wings of confused moths,
The good went to the forest.

Āsaṃsārāt tri|bhuvanam idaṃ
cinvatāṃ tātas tādṛṅ,
n' âiv' âsmākaṃ nayana|padavīṃ
śrotra|mārgaṃ gato vā,
yo 'yaṃ dhatte viṣaya|kariṇī|
gāḍha|gūḍh'|âbhimāna|
kṣībasy'ântaḥ|karaṇa|kariṇaḥ
saṃyam'|ānāya|līlām.

Yad etat: svac|chandaṃ
viharaṇam, akārpaṇyam aśanam,
sah' āryaiḥ saṃvāsaḥ,
śrutam upaśam'|âika|vrata|phalam,
mano manda|spandaṃ
bahir api, cirasy' âpi vimṛśan;
na jane kasy' âiṣā
pariṇatir udārasya tapasaḥ.

Jīrṇā eva mano|rathāś ca hṛdaye,
yātaṃ ca tad yauvanam;
hant'! âṅgeṣu guṇāś ca vandhya|phalatāṃ
yātā guṇajñair vinā;
kiṃ yuktaṃ? sahas" âbhyupaiti balavān
Kālaḥ kṛtānto 'kṣamī;
hā! jñātaṃ! Madan'|ântak'|âṅghri|yugalaṃ
muktv" âsti n' ânyā gatiḥ.

This triple-world steeped in worldly existence
We search, father, for that man
—who comes neither to our line of sight,
Nor to our path of hearing—
Who could easily place the tie of self-restraint
Onto the elephant of the mind,
Intoxicated by a deep hidden desire
For the she-elephant, object of the senses.

Everything: walking around at my leisure,
Food gained without misery,
Association with noble people,
Learning that produces the unique ritual of tranquility,
Mind extending itself slowly outside.
While I have been reflecting long,
I do not know
From what exalted austerity this is the outcome.

Desires have died in the heart,
Youth has gone in the limbs.
Alas! In the absence of connoisseurs of good qualities,
Such qualities have become useless.
What to do?
Time the destroyer, unendurable, powerful, approaches
rapidly.
Ah! I know! Except for the feet of Kama's destroyer,
There is no other refuge.

Maheśvare vā jagatām adhīśvare,
Janārdane vā jagad|antar'|ātmani:
na vastu|bheda|pratipattir asti me;
tath" âpi bhaktis taruṇ'|êndu|śekhare.

85 Sphurat sphāra|jyotsnā|
dhavalita|tale kv' âpi puline
sukh'|āsīnāḥ śānta|
dhvaniṣu rajanīṣu Dyu|saritaḥ,
bhav'|ābhog'|ôdvignāḥ
«Śiva! Śiva! Śiv'! êty» ucca|vacasaḥ;
kadā yāsyāmo 'ntar|
gata|bahula|bāṣp'|ākula|daśām?

Vitīrṇe sarasve,
taruṇa|karuṇ"|āpūrṇa|hṛdayāḥ,
smarantaḥ saṃsāre
viguṇa|pariṇāmāṃ vidhi|gatim,
vayaṃ puṇy'|âraṇye
pariṇata|sarac|candra|kariṇāḥ
tri|yāmā neṣyāmo,
Hara|caraṇa|cint"|âika|śaraṇāḥ.

Kadā Vārāṇasyām
Amara|taṭa|nīrodhasi vasan
vasānaḥ kaupīnaṃ
śirasi nidadhāno 'ñjali|puṭam,
«aye! Gaurī|nātha!
Tripurahara! Śambho! Trinayana!
prasīd'! êty» ākrośan,
nimiṣam iva neśyāmi divasān.

Either Mahéshvara is the overlord of the worlds,
Or Janárdana is the inner-self of the world.
I perceive no contradiction.
Even so, I am devoted to the god whose crest is the young
moon.

On a sandbank of the Ganges, surface blazing white, 85
Its brilliance increasing splendidly,
We happily seated,
During nights of restful sound.
Oppressed by the experiences of transient existence
Crying out loudly "Shiva! Shiva! Shiva!"
When will we reach that state
Filled with so many inner tears?

Wealth given away,
Hearts filled with fresh compassion,
We remember that course of fate,
The ripening of evil in transient existence.
In the auspicious forest
We will spend the nights,
Filled with a full autumnal moon's rays,
Our sole refuge—contemplation of Hara's feet.

When I dwell on the Ganges' bank,
In Varánasi,
Wearing a loincloth
Hands raised to the head in salutation,
"Hey! Gauri's Lord! Destroyer of Tri·pura!
Shambhu! Tri·náyana!
Favor me!" shouting out,
I will pass the days as if they were a moment.

Snātvā Gāṅgaiḥ payobhiḥ śuci|kusuma|phalair,
arcayitvā Vibhos tvām,
dhyeye dhyānaṃ niveśya, kṣiti|dhara|kuhara|
grāma|paryaṅka|mūle
ātm'|ārāmaṃ phal'|âśī guru|vacana|ratas
tvat|prasādāt Smar'|âre
duḥkhaṃ mokṣye kad" âhaṃ
sama|kara|caraṇe puṃsi sevā|samuttham?

Ekākī niḥspṛhaḥ śāntaḥ
pāṇi|pātro dig|ambaraḥ
kadā Śambho bhaviṣyāmi
karma|nirmūlana|kṣamaḥ?

90 Pāṇiṃ pātrayatāṃ, nisarga|śucinā
bhaikṣeṇa saṃtuṣyatām,
yatra kv' âpi niṣīdatāṃ, bahu|tṛṇaṃ
viśvaṃ muhuḥ paśyatām,
atyāge 'pi tanor, akhaṇḍa|param'|
ānand'|âvabodha|spṛśām
adhvā ko 'pi Śiva|prasāda|sulabhaḥ
saṃpātsyate yoginām.

Having bathed in Ganges water splendid with flowers and blossoms,
Having worshipped you, Lord,
Having entered a proper meditation,
At the base of a stone couch in a mountain cave,
Rejoicing in myself, eating fruit, devoted to the teacher's command,
When, by your favor, Enemy of Kama,
Will I release that misery
Caused by service to a tax-levying king?

Solitary, desireless, tranquil,
My hand a plate, naked.
When, Shambhu,
Will I be able to eradicate karma?

Use the hand as a cup,
Be fully satisfied with begged food, which is naturally pure,
Sit down anywhere,
Always see everything simply as grass.
Even not abandoning the body,
For yogins,
Who touch the understanding of the unfragmented highest bliss,
Any path is easily gained by Shiva's favor.

Kaupīnaṃ śata|khaṇḍa|jarjarataraṃ,
    kanthā punas tādṛśī,
naiścintyaṃ nirapekṣa|bhaikṣam aśanaṃ,
    nidrā smaśāne vane,
svātantryeṇa niraṅkuśaṃ viharaṇaṃ,
    svāntaṃ praśāntaṃ sadā,
sthairyaṃ yoga|mah"|ôtsave 'pi ca yadi:
    trailokya|rājyena kim?

Brahm"|âṇḍaṃ maṇḍalī|mātraṃ
    kiṃ lobhāya manasvinaḥ?
śapharī|sphuriten' âbdhiḥ
    kṣubdho na khalu jāyate.

Mātar Lakṣmi! bhajasva kaṃcid aparaṃ;
    mat|kāṅkṣiṇī mā sma bhūḥ;
bhogeṣu spṛhayālavas tava vaśe;
    kā niḥspṛhāṇām asi?
sadyaḥ syūta|palāśa|patra|puṭikā|
    pātre pavitrī|kṛtaiḥ
bhikṣā|vastubhir eva saṃprati vayaṃ
    vṛttiṃ samīhāmahe.

If your loincloth is of one hundred pieces of torn cloth,
Clothes of a similar kind,
Beg food disinterestedly and without concern,
Spend the night in a cemetery grove,
Wander unchecked of your own volition,
Mind always tranquil,
And firmness in yogic concentration,
What's the use of sovereignty over the triple-world?

For the reflective man
Is the creation simply a circle of greed?
The ocean is certainly not agitated
By fish flashing about.

Mother, Lakshmi! Serve some other fortunate man.
You may want me, but you will not have me.
Those who strongly yearn for worldly objects are in your
power.
What are you to those without such yearnings?
Right now, we just want a lifestyle
Of begged things,
Purified in a hollow bag
Made of sewn *palásha* leaves.

Mahā|śayyā pṛthvī,
    vipulam upadhānaṃ bhuja|latā,
vitānaṃ c' ākāśaṃ,
    vyajanam anukūlo 'yam anilaḥ,
śarac|candro dīpo,
    virati|vanitā|saṅga|muditaḥ:
sukhī śāntaḥ śete
    munir atanu|bhūtir nṛpa iva.

95 Bhikṣ"|âśī, jana|madhya|saṅga|rahitaḥ,
    sv'|āyatta|ceṣṭaḥ sadā,
hān'|ādāna|virakta|mārga|nirataḥ,
    kaś cit tapasvī sthitaḥ,
rathy'|ākīrṇa|viśīrṇa|jīrṇa|vasanaḥ
    saṃprāpta|kanth"|āsanaḥ,
nirmāno nirahaṃkṛtiḥ śama|sukh'|
    ābhog'|âika|baddha|spṛhaḥ.

Caṇḍālaḥ kim ayaṃ dvi|jātir athavā
    śūdro 'tha kiṃ tāpasaḥ?
kiṃ vā tattva|viveka|peśala|matir
    yog'|īśvaraḥ ko 'pi kim?
ity utpanna|vikalpa|jalpa|mukharair
    ābhāṣyamāṇā janaiḥ
na kruddhāḥ pathi n' âiva tuṣṭa|manaso
    yānti svayaṃ yoginaḥ.

His huge bed is the ground,
His long arm a broad pillow,
The sky for a canopy,
The pleasant wind a fan,
The autumn moon his lamp,
His delight, attachment to the woman called
 indifference.
Easily sleeps the tranquil ascetic,
Like the prosperous king.

Eating begged food, detached from crowds, 95
Always acting as befits himself,
Focussed on the path of indifference to giving and
 receiving,
A certain ascetic lived.
His garment made of old, torn clothes strewn along the
 road,
Seated on a rag he had found,
Without pride, without ego,
Desire fixed only on the pleasure of the happiness of
 repose.

Is this ascetic a despised outcaste,
A brahmin or a *shudra*?
Is his mind clever in discernment of the real
Or is he a Lord of yogins?
When people speak like this,
Their prattle and gossip forced from their imaginations,
Yogins go their own way,
Neither angered nor content in their mind.

Hinsā|śūnyam a|yatna|labhyam aśanam
    Dhātrā marut|kalpitam
vyālānām; paśavas tṛṇ"|âṅkura|bhujas
    tuṣṭāḥ sthalī|śāyinaḥ;
saṃsār'|ârṇava|laṅghana|kṣama|dhiyām
    vṛttiḥ kṛtā sā nṛṇām;
tām anveṅayatāṃ prayānti satataṃ
    sarve samāptiṃ guṇāḥ.

Gaṅgā|tīre Hima|giri|śilā|
    baddha|padm'|āsanasya
Brahma|dhyān'|âbhyasana|vidhinā
    yoga|nidrāṃ gatasya,
kiṃ tair bhāvyaṃ mama sudivasair,
    yatra te nirviśaṅkāḥ
kaṇṣūyante jaraṭha|hariṇāḥ
    sv'|âṅgam aṅge madīye?

Pāṇiḥ pātraṃ pavitraṃ, bhramaṇa|parigataṃ
    bhaikṣam akṣayyam annam,
vistīrṇaṃ vastram āśā|daśakam, acapalaṃ
    talpam asvalpam Ūrvī
yeṣāṃ; niḥsaṅgat"|âṅgī|karaṇa|pariṇata|
    svānta|saṃtoṣinas te
dhanyāḥ saṃnyasta|dainya|vyatikara|nikarāḥ
    karma nirmūlayanti.

Brahma created the wind as food for snakes.
It is gained without effort and peacefully.
Animals are satisfied eating blades of grass
And sleeping on an unprepared ground.
He created a lifestyle for men
With minds able to cross the sea of transient existence.
Those searching for it
Always have their qualities fulfilled.

When on the Ganges' bank
On a Himalayan crag in the lotus position
Practicing meditation on Brahma
I achieved the sleep of yoga,
What will I accomplish
During these days
Of old deer fearlessly
Scratching their body on my body?

My hand a pure container, alms gained by wandering,
Inexhaustible food,
Clothes spread everywhere,
Huge immovable bed the Earth.
Those fortunate men,
Hearts' satisfied by the transformation urged from
non-attachment,
Mixed multitude of misery abandoned,
Eradicate karma.

100 Mātar Medini! tāta māruta! sakhe
tejaḥ! subandho jala!
bhrātar vyoman! nibaddha eva bhavatām
antyaḥ praṇām'|âñjaliḥ.
yuṣmat|saṅga|vaś'|ôpajāta|sukṛta|
sphāra|sphuran|nirmala|
jñān'|âpāsta|samasta|moha|mahimā
līye para|Brahmaṇi.

Mother Earth! Father wind! Friend fire! 100
Dear kinsman water!
Brother air! To you finally the offering of hands cupped together.
The entire abundance of delusion
Has disappeared through the pure knowledge
Sparkling everywhere by the good karma sprung up from attachment to you.
I cling to the supreme Brahma.

ÁMARU: HUNDRED VERSES

Jy"|ākṛṣṭi|baddha|khaṭakā|mukha|pāṇi|pṛṣṭha|
preṅkhan|nakh'|âṅśu|caya|saṃvalito 'mbikāyāḥ
tvāṃ pātu mañjarita|pallava|karṇapūra|
lobha|bhramad|bhramara|vibhrama|bhṛt|kaṭākṣaḥ!

Kṣipto hast'|âvalagnaḥ, prasabham abhihato
'py ādadāno 'ṅśuk'|ântaṃ,
gṛhṇan keśeṣv apāstaś, caraṇa|nipatito
n' ēkṣitaḥ saṃbhrameṇa,
āliṅgan yo 'vadhūtas tripura|yuvatibhiḥ,
s'|âśru|netr'|ôtpalābhiḥ
kām" îv' ārdr'|âparādhaḥ. Sa dahatu duritam
Śāmbhavo vaḥ śar'|âgniḥ.

Splendid as the bees
Wandering greedily around her ear bouquet,
Ámbika's glance has
co-mingled
With radiant nails
Reflecting upon the back of her hand
Tensed in *khátaka·mukha* mode
For drawing the bow.
May it protect you!

The fire of Shiva's arrow,
Clung to the hands of the women of the triple-city,
Lotus-eyes teary.
They cast it aside.
Though struck hard
It returns to the hem of their dresses.
Yet repelled,
Seizes their hair.
Still, lapping at their feet.
Is not seen in their agitation.
Embraces them,
Even then spurned,
As a lover who just had another woman.
May it burn away our evil.

Ālolām alak'|āvalīṃ vilulitāṃ
    bibhrac, calat|kuṇḍalam,
kiṃ|cin|mṛṣṭa|viśeṣakaṃ tanutaraiḥ
    sved'|âmbhasaḥ śīkaraiḥ,
tanvyā yat surat'|ânta|tānta|nayanaṃ
    vaktraṃ rati|vyatyaye,
tat tvāṃ pātu cirāya! kiṃ Hari|Hara|
    Skand'|ādibhir devataiḥ?

Alasa|valitaiḥ
    prem'|ârdr'|ârdrair muhur mukulī|kṛtaiḥ
kṣaṇam abhimukhair
    lajj"|ālolair nimeṣa|parāṅmukhaiḥ
hṛdaya|nihitaṃ
    bhāv'|ākūtaṃ vamadbhir iv' ēkṣaṇaiḥ:
kathaya, sukṛtī
    ko 'yaṃ, mugdhe, tvay" âdya vilokyate?

Of a slender woman,
Lovemaking just completed in the male position,
Her face
  Eyes languid at the end of sex
  Bindu almost removed by a subtle spray of moisture
  Shaking earrings
  Dishevelled tendrils of hair
May it long protect you.
Gods—Vishnu, Shiva and Skanda—
Are useless.

Rolling languidly,
Moist with fresh love
Closed repeatedly like a bud
  Facing for an instant
Tentative in embarrassment
Unblinking,
  Almost forcing out
The incipient signs of love
Fixed in your heart.
Who is this lucky man those eyes have seen?
Tell me now, artless woman.

5 Aṅguly|agra|nakhena bāṣpa|salilaṃ vikṣipya
vikṣipya, kim
tūṣṇīṃ rodiṣī kopane? bahutaraṃ
phūt|kṛtya rodiṣyasi,
yasyās te piśun'|ôpadeśa|vacanair
māne 'tibhūmiṃ gate
nirviṇṇo 'nunayaṃ prati priyatamo
madhyasthatām eṣyati.

Datto 'syāḥ praṇayas tvay" âiva, bhavat"
âiv' êyaṃ ciraṃ lālitā;
daivād adya kila tvam eva kṛtavān
asyā navaṃ vipriyam;
manyur duḥsaha eva yāty upaśamaṃ
no sāntva|vādaiḥ sphuṭam.
he nistriṅśa! vimukta|kaṇṭha|karuṇaṃ
tāvat sakhī roditu.

Likhann āste bhūmiṃ
bahir avanataḥ prāṇa|dayitaḥ;
nirāhārāḥ sakhyaḥ
satata|rudit'|ôcchūna|nayanāḥ;
parityaktaṃ sarvaṃ
hasita|paṭhitaṃ pañjara|śukaiḥ;
tav' âvasthā c' êyaṃ:
visṛja kaṭhine mānam adhunā!

Are you weeping silently, angry woman? 5
Constantly dabbing away a rush of tears
With the tips of your nails.
You will sob much more
Now that your wounded pride
Has gone to excess
Following some malicious advice.
Your lover—despairing
Of trying to make up—
Will become indifferent.

You surely gave her your love,
You surely cherished her long.
Now by fate, it seems,
You have betrayed her.
Such rage cannot be overcome
It is plainly not to be appeased by conciliatory words.
Ungrateful man!
Long will my friend freely weep pitiable tears.

He sits outside, writing on the ground,
    bowed down, the love of your life.
Your friends are famished,
    eyes swollen by constant weeping.
The caged parrots
their mirth and mimicry totally ceased.
And this is your plight.
Get rid of your wounded pride
Now, obdurate woman.

Nāryo mugdha|śaṭhā haranti ramaṇaṃ,
tiṣṭhanti no vāritāḥ;
tat kiṃ tāmyasi? kiṃ ca rodiṣi mudhā?
tāsāṃ priyaṃ mā kṛthāḥ!
kāntaḥ keli|rucir yuvā sahṛdayas
tādṛk patiḥ, kātare,
kiṃ no barbara|karkaśaiḥ? priya|śatair
ākramya vikrīyate.

Kopāt komala|lola|bāhu|latikā|
pāśena baddhvā dṛḍhaṃ,
nītvā vāsa|niketanaṃ dayitayā
sāyaṃ sakhīnāṃ puraḥ,
«bhūyo 'py evam! iti» skhalan mṛdu|girā
saṃsūcya duśceṣṭitam,
dhanyo hanyata eva nihnuti|paraḥ
preyān rudatyā hasan.

10 «Yātāḥ kiṃ na milanti, sundari, punaś?
cintā tvayā mat|kṛte
no kāryā! nitarāṃ kṛś" âsi» kathayaty
evaṃ sa|bāṣpe mayi;
lajjā|manthara|tārakeṇa nipatat|
pīt'|âśruṇā cakṣuṣā
dṛṣṭvā māṃ, hasitena bhāvi|maraṇ'|
ôtsāhas tayā sūcitas.

Those women, deceitfully innocent, are stealing your love.
They will not be stopped.
Why give in?
Why weep in vain?
Don't humor them!
Handsome, sensual, young, a sophisticate,
Such is your husband, timid woman.
Why should we use hard vulgarities?
Win him over with a hundred sweet words.
He'll change.

Angrily his lover bound him tight
With bonds—soft, creeper-like arms,
Led him at evening to the bedroom
In front of her friends,
Hinted as his misdemeanor
In sweet hesitant words, "This, still once more."
The weeping woman strikes the lucky lover
Who laughs—an adept at betrayal.

"Won't those who have gone abroad meet again, beautiful 10
woman?
Don't be anxious about me!
You're terribly thin,"
I said, teary.
With her eyes spilling tears,
pupils languid with shame,
She watched me, laughed and indicated
Her rash resolve of imminent death.

Tad|vaktr'|âbhimukhaṃ mukhaṃ vinamitaṃ,
    dṛṣṭiḥ kṛtā pādayos,
tasy' ālāpa|kutūhal'|ākulatara|
    śrotre niruddhe mayā,
pāṇibhyāṃ ca tiraskṛtaḥ sa|pulakaḥ
    sved'|ôdgamo gaṇḍayoḥ;
sakhyaḥ, kiṃ karavāṇi, yānti śatadhā
    yat kañcuke saṃdhayaḥ?

«Prahara|viratau,
    madhye v" âhnas tato 'pi pareṇa vā,
kim uta sakale
    yāte v" âhni, priya, tvam ih' âiṣyasi?»
iti dina|śata|
    prāpyaṃ deśaṃ priyasya yiyāsataḥ
harati gamanaṃ
    bāl" ālāpaiḥ sa|bāṣpa|galaj|jalaiḥ.

Dhīraṃ vāri|dharasya vāri kirataḥ
    śrutvā niśīthe dhvanim,
dīrgh'|ôcchvāsam udaśruṇā virāhiṇīṃ
    bālāṃ ciraṃ dhyāyatā,
adhvanyena vimukta|kaṇṭham akhilāṃ
    rātriṃ tathā kranditam,
grāmīṇaiḥ punar adhvagasya vasatir
    grāme niṣiddhā yathā.

When my face faced his I bowed it,
My eyes directed at his feet,
My ears—desperate to hear his talk
I blocked.
Moist cheeks and goose bumps
My hands concealed.
Friends, what must I do?
When the joins of my bodice
Are breached one hundred-fold.

"Will it be in the first part of the night,
In the middle, or somewhat later,
Or when the day is entirely gone
That you return, lover?"
These words gushing with tears,
The young woman delays the departure of her lover,
Yearning to leave for a country
One hundred days away.

At midnight he hears the thunderclouds' deep roar
Of cascading water,
And sighing deeply, tearful,
Long contemplating the young woman from whom he is separated,
The traveller wailed so freely
All night
That the villagers no longer permitted
Any wayfarer to stay in the village.

Kṛto dūrād eva
smita|madhuram abhyudgama|vidhiḥ,
śirasy ājñā nyastā
prativacanavaty ānatimati,
na dṛṣṭeḥ śaithilyaṃ
milana iti ceto dahati me;
nigūḍh'|ântaḥ|kopā,
kaṭhina|hṛdaye, saṃvṛtir iyam.

15 Katham api, sakhi,
krīḍā|kopād «vraj' êti» may" ôdite;
kaṭhina|hṛdayaḥ
śayyāṃ tyaktvā, balād gata eva saḥ.
iti sa|rabhasaṃ
dhvasta|premṇi vyapeta|ghṛṇe spṛhām;
punar api hata|
vrīḍaṃ cetaḥ karoti; karomi kim?

Dampatyor niśi jalpator gṛha|śuken'
ākarṇitaṃ yad vacaḥ,
tat prātar guru|saṃnidhau nigadataḥ
śrutv" âiva, tāraṃ vadhūḥ
karṇ'|ālambita|padma|rāga|śakalaṃ
vinyasya cañcvāḥ puraḥ,
vrīḍ"|ārtā prakaroti dāḍima|phala|
vyājena vāg|bandhanam.

As was the custom, she rose up from afar
Smiling sweetly,
Responded deferentially to my command,
Her head bowed,
Slackened not her gaze at the meeting.
But all this burns my heart.
This is deception veiling the anger
In your heart. Callous woman!

Hardly friend, when angrily—but really in fun— 15
"Go," I said,
Then the cruel man just left the bed,
Went.
Now his love has shattered instantly,
His recollection dispersed.
Still, for him yearns my shameless heart.
What can I do?

Of two lovers chattering in the night
A house parrot heard the conversation,
Which, morning come, it utters too shrilly near the young bride's parents
Hearing this,
She placed a piece of ruby—a semblance of a pomegranate fruit—
from her ear before his beak.
For sick with shame
She contrives to block his speech.

Ajñānena parāṅmukhīṃ paribhavād
āśliṣya māṃ duḥkhitām;
kiṃ labdham, śaṭha, durnayena nayatā
saubhāgyam etāṃ daśām?
paśy' âitad dayitā|kuca|vyatikar'|
ônmṛṣṭ'|âṅga|rāg'|âruṇam
vakṣas te mala|taila|paṅka|śabalair
veṇī|padair aṅkitam!

Ekatr' āsana|saṃsthitiḥ parihṛtā
pratyudgamād dūrataḥ;
tāmbūl'āharaṇa|chalena rabhas"
āśleṣo 'pi saṃvighnitaḥ;
ālāpo 'pi na miśritaḥ parijanaṃ
vyāpārayanty" ântike
kāntaṃ pratyupacārataś caturayā
kopaḥ kṛt'|ârthīkṛtaḥ.

Dṛṣṭv" âik'|āsana|saṃsthite priyatame,
paścād upety' ādarād,
ekasyā nayane nimīlya vihita|
krīḍ"|ânubandha|chalaḥ,
īśad|vakrita|kandharaḥ sa|pulakaḥ
prem'|ôllasan|mānasām
antar|hāsa|lasat|kapola|phalakāṃ
dhūrto 'parāṃ cumbati.

You have embraced me boorishly
With my back turned and pained by your insult.
Rogue! What is gained from this impudence,
Reducing your conjugal delight to this state?
Look! Your chest! It's red with ointment
Rubbed off your lover's breasts during love-play
And marked with the imprint of braided hair
Flecked with unguent and oil.

By rising to meet him coming in the distance
She escaped sitting with him on the same seat.
By pretending to bring some betel
Frustrated his passionate embrace.
By keeping her retinue occupied nearby
Not even conversation was entertained.
Her behavior to her husband may be appropriate,
By her craft her anger has reached its goal.

His two lovely women on the same seat he saw,
Crept up carefully from behind,
Closed the eyes of one
Pretending the required love-play.
And—his neck slightly bent
The rascal kisses the other woman
Whose heart radiates love,
Cheeks glowing from inner laughter.

20 Caraṇa|patana|
pratyākhyāna|prasāda|parāṅmukhe,
«nibhṛta|kitav'|
ācār' êty» ukte ruṣā paruṣī|kṛte,
vrajati ramaṇe,
niḥśvasy' ôccaiḥ, stan'|ârpita|hastayā
nayana|salila|
cchannā dṛṣṭiḥ sakhīṣu nipātitā.

«Kāñcyā gāḍhatar'|âvanaddha|vasana|
prāntā kim arthaṃ punar
mugdh"|âkṣī svapit' îti?» tat parijanaṃ
svairaṃ priye pṛcchati,
«mātaḥ, svaptum ap' îha vārayati mām»
ity āhita|krodhayā
paryasya svapana|chalena śayane
datto 'vakāśas tayā.

Ekasmiñ śayane vipakṣa|ramaṇī|
nāma|grahe mugdhayā
sadyaḥ kopa|parāṅ|mukhaṃ glapitayā
cāṭūni kurvann api;
āvegād avadhīritaḥ priyatamas
tūṣṇīṃ sthitas tat|kṣaṇād,
mā bhūn mlāna iv' êty amanda|valita|
grīvaṃ punar vīkṣitaḥ.

Forbade him falling at her feet
So he was unresponsive to her favor
Angrily told "You're a sly cheat,"
So he felt slighted.
And when her lover leaves,
Sighing heavily, hand on her breast,
Her face
    eyes obscured by a torrent of tears
Is fixed on her friends.

When her lover softly asks her retinue,
"Why is this woman of trembling eyes asleep again?
She has the end of her sari
Drawn so tight on her waist band,"
"Mother, he still stops me sleeping,"
She expostulates angrily,
Throwing herself around in a pretense of sleep,
Making a place on the bed.

He mentions a rival woman's name
When they are together on the same bed.
Languid, the delicate girl instantly turns away in anger
While he makes excuses.
Flustered, her lover, rejected,
Stayed silent, until,
Instantly,
As if he might wither away,
Rapidly turned her neck,
Looked again.

Ekasmiñ śayane parāṅmukhatayā
    vīt'|ôttaraṃ tāmyatoḥ,
anyonyaṃ hṛdaya|sthite 'py anunaye,
    saṃrakṣator gauravam;
daṃpatyoḥ śanakair apāṅga|valanān
    miśrī|bhavac|cakṣuṣoḥ,
bhagno māna|kaliḥ, sahāsa|rabhasaṃ
    vyāvṛtta|kaṇṭha|grahaḥ.

«Paśyāmo mayi kiṃ prapadyata iti»
    sthairyaṃ may" ālambitam;
«kiṃ māṃ n' ālapat" îty? ayaṃ khalu śaṭhaḥ»
    kopas tay" âpy āśritaḥ;
ity anyonya|vilakṣa|dṛṣṭi|cature
    tasminn avasth"|ântare,
savyājaṃ hasitaṃ mayā, dhṛti|haro
    bāṣpas tu muktas tayā.

25 Parimlāne māne,
    mukha|śaśini tasyāḥ kara|dhṛte,
mayi kṣīṇ'|ôpāye
    praṇipatana|mātr'|âika|śaraṇe;
tayā pakṣma|prānta|
    dhvaja|puṭa|niruddhena sahasā
prasādo bāṣpeṇa
    stana|taṭa|viśīrṇena kathitaḥ.

On a single bed, backs turned,
Without conversation, depressed,
And even if forgiveness stands in each of their hearts
They stand on their own dignity.
For that husband and wife,
Gradually—a turning of the eye,
Their eyes intertwine,
Love's quarrel is broken,
And laughing, energetically,
They embrace—facing each other.

"Let's see what happens to me," I wondered.
I put on a serious guise.
"Why doesn't he talk to me. He's a rogue."
And she remained angry.
While our eyes enchantingly darted
    in no direction in this standoff,
I feigned laughter,
But she lost her resolve and released a tear.

When her angry pride was exhausted 25
Her moon-like face held in her hand,
My strategies had failed,
My last resort just to bow at her feet.
Suddenly, using her palms as emblems
    at the corners of her eyes,
She blocked
A tear, until it shattered on her breast.
Thus was her favor signalled.

«Tasyāḥ sāndra|vilepana|stana|yuga|
praśleṣa|mudr"|âṅkitam
kiṃ vakṣaś caraṇ'|ānati|vyatikara|
vyājena gopāyyate?»
ity ukte «kva tad?» ity udīrya, sahasā
tat sampramārṣṭuṃ mayā
s" āśliṣṭā rabhasena, tat|sukha|vaśāt
tasyāś ca tad vismṛtam.

«Tvaṃ mugdh'|âkṣī vin" âiva kañculikayā
dhatse manohāriṇīm
lakṣmīm ity» abhidhāyini priyatame,
tad|vīṭikā|saṃspṛśi;
śayy'|ôpānta|niviṣṭa|sasmita|sakhī|
netr'|ôtsav'|ānanditaḥ
niryātaḥ śanakair alīka|vacan'|
ôpanyāsam ālī|janaḥ.

Bhrū|bhaṅge racite 'pi dṛṣṭir adhikaṃ
s'|ôtkaṇṭham udvīkṣate;
ruddhāyām api vāci, sa|smitam idaṃ
dagdh'|ānanaṃ jāyate;
kārkaśyaṃ gamite 'pi cetasi, tanuḥ
romāñcam ālambate;
dṛṣṭe nirvahaṇaṃ bhaviṣyati kathaṃ
mānasya tasmiñ jane?

"You're hiding your chest
By pretending to bow at my feet. Why?
It is stamped by the tight
Embrace of her two oiled breasts."
This being said, I said, "Where is it?,"
    and to wipe it away
Embraced her passionately.
And under its spell of happiness
She forgot about it.

"Woman of the tremulous eyes,
Without your upper garment
You are enchantingly beautiful,"
Her dearest said while fiddling with its knot.
Delighted at the joy in the eye of her smiling friend
Seated on the bed's edge,
The friend contrived some excuse,
Quietly left.

Her brows might be contracted
But she looks up longingly.
Her voice might have stopped,
But her pained face assumes a smile.
Her heart might have become hard,
But her body thrills.
How can she hold her angry pride
If that man appears?

Sā patyuḥ pratham'âparādha|samaye
sakhy'|ôpadeśaṃ vinā
no jānāti sa|vibhram'|âṅga|valanā|
vakr'|ôkti|saṃsūcanam;
svacchair accha|kapola|mūla|galitaiḥ
paryasta|netr'|ôtpalā
bālā kevalam eva roditi luṭhal|
lol'|ôdakair aśrubhiḥ.

30 Bhavatu, viditaṃ.
vyarth'|ālāpair alaṃ, priya! gamyatām!
tanur api na te,
doṣo 'smākaṃ vidhis tu parāṅmukhaḥ
tava yadi tath"
ārūḍhaṃ prema prapannam imāṃ daśām,
prakṛti|tarale
kā naḥ pīḍā gate hata|jīvite?

Urasi nihitas
tāro hāraḥ, kṛtā jaghane ghane
kala|kalavatī
kāñcīm pādau raman|maṇī|nūpurau:
priyam abhisarasy
evaṃ, mugdhe! tvam āhata|ḍiṇḍimā
yadi kim adhika|
trās'|ôtkampaṃ diśaḥ samudīkṣase?

The time of her husband's first betrayal,
She bereft of her friends' advice,
Ignorant of the deceptive signals
Created by rolling her body coquettishly.
Her lotus-like eyes flickering about,
All the young girl does is weep
Tears crystal clear and meandering,
Flowing right down her bright cheeks.

I know now. Stop this ridiculous chatter! 30
Lover, go!
No fault rests on you.
Fate is hostile toward me.
Since your love—to have scaled such heights,
Has reached this state,
What is pain to me,
Seeing that my life—devastated now—
Fickle by nature, has gone?

On her breast rested a shining string of pearls,
On her firm hips a tinkling girdle fixed,
Her feet, jewelled anklets jingling.
So you approach your lover, delicate woman,
Like a loudly beaten drum.
If so, why look about
Trembling fearfully?

Malaya|marutāṃ
  vrātā vātā, vikāsita|mallikā|
parimala|bharo
  bhagno grīṣmas, tvam utsahase yadi,
ghana! ghaṭayituṃ
  taṃ niḥsnehaṃ ya eva nivartane
prabhavati gavāṃ;
  kiṃ naś chinnaṃ? sa eva Dhanañjayaḥ.

Prātaḥ|prātar upāgatena janitā
  nirnidratā cakṣuṣoḥ;
mandāyā mama gauravaṃ vyapagataṃ,
  protpāditaṃ lāghavam;
kiṃ tad yan na kṛtaṃ tvayā? maraṇabhīr
  muktā, mayā gamyatām;
duḥkhaṃ tiṣṭhasi; yac ca pathyam adhunā
  kart" âsmi, tad śroṣyasi.

Sā bālā, vayam apragalbha|manasaḥ;
  sā strī, vayaṃ kātarāḥ;
sā pīn'|ônnatimat|payodhara|yugaṃ
  dhatte, sa|khedā vayam;
s" ākrāntā jaghana|sthalena guruṇā,
  gantuṃ na śaktā vayaṃ;
doṣair anya|jan'|āśrayair apaṭavo
  jātāḥ sma ity, adbhutam!

Malabar winds' hosts have blown,
Jasmine's weighty fragrance diffused,
Summer is broken.
Cloud, maybe you can
Bring back that loveless man.
But what is it to me?
Whoever can drive the cows home,
He is my Dhanañ·jaya.

Every morning you arrived
Sleep departed my eyes
Heaviness retreated from my spirit.
Light have I been made.
What else could you have done?
Fear of death has left me.
So go! You are unsettled.
What I do now for my health
You will hear.

She is young, my heart demure.
She is a woman, I timid.
She has full breasts bowed down,
I am depressed.
She has triumphed with her abundant thighs,
I cannot leave.
My lack of skill with another person
Has made me clumsy. Amazing!

35 Prasthānaṃ valayaiḥ kṛtaṃ, priyasakhair
asrair ajasraṃ gatam,
dhṛtyā na kṣaṇam āsitaṃ, vyavasitaṃ
cittena gantuṃ puraḥ;
yātuṃ niścita|cetasi priyatame,
sarve samaṃ prasthitā;
gantavye sati, jīvita, priya|suhṛt|
sārthaḥ kim u tyajyate?

Saṃdaṣṭe 'dhara|pallave, sacakitaṃ
hast'|âgram ādhunvatī:
«mā! mā! muñca śaṭh'! êti» kopa|vacanair
ānartita|bhrū|latā,
sītkār'|âñcita|locanā sarabhasaṃ;
yaiś cumbitā māninī,
prāptaṃ tair amṛtam, śramāya mathito
mūḍhaiḥ suraiḥ sāgaraḥ.

«Supto 'yaṃ, sakhi! supyatām iti» gatāḥ
sakhyas, tato 'nantaram:
prem'|âveśitayā mayā saralayā
nyastaṃ mukhaṃ tan|mukhe;
jñāte 'līka|nimīlane nayanayor
dhūrtasya romāñcataḥ;
lajj" āsīn mama, tena s" âpy apahṛtā
tat|kāla|yogyaiḥ kramaiḥ.

My bracelets gone, 35
My tears, dear friends, flowed incessant,
My resolve lasted but a moment,
My mind resolved to go first.
When my love decided to leave
Everything left together.
Life, if you must go,
Why leave your retinue of friends?

When her lower lip was bitten,
Shakes her finger in alarm.
"No! No! Release me, rogue!," and such angry words
Danced her creeper-like brows.
Then she curled her eyes with an intake of breath.
Whoever impetuously kissed that proud woman
Tasted ambrosia: for this the stupid gods
Churned the ocean exhaustion.

"He is asleep, friend! You must sleep."
So saying her friends left. Then an opportunity.
Overpowered by love my mouth I placed
Right on his.
Then it struck me. The rogue's skin had arisen,
He had just feigned closing his eyes.
I was ashamed, but that too he swept away
With advances proper for the moment.

Kopo yatra bhrū|kuṭi|racanā,
    nigraho yatra maunam,
yatr' ânyonya|smitam anunayo,
    dṛṣṭi|pātaḥ prasādaḥ;
tasya premṇas tad idam adhunā
    vaiśasaṃ paśya jātam!
tvaṃ pād'|ânte luṭhasi, na ca me
    manyu|mokṣaḥ khalāyāḥ.

«Sutanu, jahihi maunaṃ!
    paśya pād'ānataṃ mām!
na khalu tava kadācit
    kopa evaṃ|vidho 'bhūt.»
iti nigadati nāthe,
    tiryag|āmīlit'|âkṣyā
nayana|jalam analpaṃ
    muktam, uktaṃ na kiṃ cit.

40 Gāḍh'|āliṅgana|vāmanī|kṛta|kuca|
    proddhūta|rom'|ôdgamā,
sāndra|sneha|ras'|âtireka|vigalac|
    chrīman|nitamb'|âmbarā:
«mā! mā! mānada! m" âti mām alam! iti»
    kṣām'|âkṣar'|ôllāpinī;
suptā kiṃ nu, mṛtā nu kiṃ, manasi kiṃ
    līnā, vilīnā nu kim?

Anger—a mere raising of the brow.
Disagreement—mere silence.
Making up—a mutual smile.
Favor—a passing glance.
But now, look!
Love ruined.
You grovel at my feet,
But wilful as I am, my anger is not released.

"Slender woman. Drop your silence!
Look! At your feet I am bowed.
Never was your anger
Such as this."
Her husband declared,
Eyes cast down.
One huge droplet her eye released,
Nothing said.

Her breasts flattened by tight embrace, 40
Her skin has thrilled.
From love's excessive exudation
Slips the garment on her lustrous hips.
"No! No! Breaker of pride! Absolutely no more,"
She pleads weakly.
Was she asleep, or dead,
Melted into my heart or just dissolved?

Paṭ'ālagne patyau,
namayati mukhaṃ jāta|vinayā;
haṭh'|āśleṣaṃ vāñchaty,
apaharati gātrāṇi nibhṛtam;
na śaknoty ākhyātuṃ,
smita|mukha|sakhī|datta|nayanā;
hriyā tāmyaty antaḥ
prathama|parihāse nava|vadhūḥ.

N' âpeto 'nunayena yaḥ, priya|suhṛd|
vākyair na yaḥ saṃhṛtaḥ,
yo dīrghaṃ divasaṃ viṣahya viṣamaṃ
yatnāt kathaṃcid dhṛtaḥ,
anyonyasya hṛte mukhe nihitayos
tiryak kathaṃ cid dṛśoḥ,
sa dvābhyām ativismṛta|vyatikaro
māno vihasy' ôjjhitaḥ.

Gate prem'|ābandhe,
praṇaya|bahumāne vigalite,
nivṛtte sadbhāve
jana iva jane gacchati puraḥ;
tad utprekṣy' ôtprekṣya,
priya|sakhi, gatāṃs tāṃś ca divasān, na
na jāne ko hetur
dalati śatadhā yan na hṛdayam.

Her husband—clings to the sari's border,
The modest woman—bows her head.
He—wants a forceful embrace.
She—silently draws her limbs away.
She cannot describe it,
Her eyes convey it to her friend, who smiles.
In her shyness the new bride
Stiffens inwardly at the first attempt at love.

It did not disappear by affection,
Was not removed by friend's heartfelt words.
It was somehow sustained
—admittedly with difficulty...
For the long day.
But when their eyes glance
Onto faces drawn toward each other
Wounded honor, mutually forgotten,
Is cast aside.

Love's tie has gone,
Loving respect slipped away,
The man's genuine emotion has receded,
He walks past—just a man.
On that focussing constantly
And on days passed, dear friend,
I do not know why
My heart does not burst into one hundred pieces.

Cira|virahiṇor
atyutkaṇṭh'|âślathī|kṛta|gātrayoḥ,
navam iva jagaj
jātaṃ, bhūyaś cirād abhinandatoḥ;
katham iva dine
dīrghe yāte, niśām adhirūḍhayoḥ;
prasarati kathā
bahvī dūnor yathā na tathā ratiḥ.

45 Dīrghā vandana|mālikā viracitā
dṛṣṭy" âiva, n' êndīvaraiḥ;
puṣpāṇāṃ prakaraḥ smitena racito,
no kunda|jāty|ādibhiḥ;
dattaḥ sveda|mucā payo|dhara|bhareṇ'
ârgho, na kumbh'|âmbhasā:
svair ev' âvayavaiḥ priyasya viśatas
tanvyā kṛtaṃ maṅgalam.

Kānte sāgasi śāpite, priya|sakhī|
veṣaṃ vidhāy' āgate,
bhrānty" āliṅgya, mayā rahasyam uditaṃ
tat|saṅgam'|ākāṅkṣayā;
«mugdhe! duṣkaram etad, ity» atitarām
uddāma|hāsaṃ balāt
āśliṣya, chalit" âsmi tena kitaven',
âdya pradoṣ'|āgame.

Long separated,
Limbs languid with ardor,
The world becomes anew
When they greet each other repeatedly.
Somehow when the long day goes
They attain night.
Of that miserable couple so much talk flows
Lovemaking there is not.

The long flower garland—woven by her eyes, 45
Not with blue lotus.
The strew of flowers—fashioned of a smile,
Not with Kunda flowers.
Water for the guest—offered from the moisture of heavy
breasts,
Not with water from a pot.
The auspicious reception for the entering lover—made
by the slender woman,
With her own body.

When the guilty lover sworn to stay away
Returned in the guise of a dear friend,
I embraced him mistakenly, whispered secretly
That I still yearned to see him.
"Delicate woman! That's too bad," said he,
Laughing loudly, embracing me impetuously.
Cheated I am by that rogue
Now night has fallen.

Āśaṅkya praṇatiṃ paṭ'|ânta|pihitau
pādau karoty ādarāt,
vyājen' āgatam āvṛṇoti hasitaṃ,
na spṛṣṭam udvīkṣate,
mayy ālapavati pratīpa|vacanaṃ
sakhyā sah' ābhāṣate;
tanvyās tiṣṭhatu nirbhara|praṇayitā
māno 'pi ramy'|ôdayaḥ.

Yāvanty eva padāny alīka|vacanair
ālī|janaiḥ pāṭhitā,
tāvanty eva kṛt'|âgaso drutataraṃ
saṃlapya patyuḥ puraḥ;
prārebhe parato yathā Manasijasy'
ēcchā tathā varṇitum:
premṇo maugdhya|vibhūṣaṇasya sahajaḥ
ko 'py eṣa kāntaḥ kramaḥ.

Dūrād utsukam āgate vivalitaṃ,
saṃbhāṣiṇi sphāritam,
saṃśliṣyaty aruṇaṃ, gṛhīta|vasane
kop'|âñcita|bhrū|latam,
māninyāś caraṇ'|ānati|vyatikare
bāṣp'|âmbu|pūrn'|ēkṣaṇam:
cakṣur jātam aho prapañca|caturaṃ
jāt" âgasi preyasi!

Anticipating my bow
She carefully covers her feet,
Conceals artfully an incipient smile,
Does not look up straight at me
If I speak,
Begins a different conversation with her girlfriend.
Filled with love as she is
Even that woman's wounded pride brings delight.

So many words in lying accusation
By her false friends instructed
Did she quickly repeat
In her unfaithful husband's presence.
Afterward, consistent with Love's desire
Does she comport herself.
Of love whose ornament is naïveté,
Here is the innate and beautiful way.

On his eager arrival from afar—turned away.
Speaking—all awonder.
Embracing her—reddens.
Seizing her sari—eyebrows angrily arched.
Bowing at the feet of that prideful woman—
Fills with tears.
Behold!—Her eye has become
Skilled in fitting itself to her lover's guilt.

50 «Aṅgānām atitānavaṃ kuta idaṃ?
kasmād akasmād idaṃ,
mugdhe, pāṇḍu|kapolam ānanam iti?»
Prāṇ'|ēśvare pṛcchati,
tanvyā «sarvam idaṃ svabhāvata iti»
vyāhṛtya, pakṣm'|ântara|
vyāpī bāṣpa|bharas tayā valitayā
niḥśvasya mukto 'nyataḥ.

Puras tanvyā, gotra|
skhalana|cakito, 'haṃ nata|mukhaḥ,
pravṛtto vailakṣyāt
kim api likhituṃ daiva|hatakaḥ.
sphuṭo rekhā|nyāsaḥ
katham api sa tādṛk pariṇato,
gatā yena vyaktiṃ
punar avayavaiḥ s" âiva taruṇī;

Tataś c' âbhijñāya
sphurad|aruṇa|gaṇḍa|sthala|rucā
manasvinyā rūḍha|
praṇaya|sahas"| ôdgadgada|girā,
«aho citraṃ! citraṃ
sphuṭam! iti» nigady' âśru|kaluṣam,
ruṣā Brahm'âstraṃ me
śirasi nihito vāma|caraṇaḥ.

"Why is your body so slender? 50
Is there a cause or is it chance?
Delicate woman! Why are your cheeks so pale?"
So the Lord of life asks.
"This is entirely by nature,"
Saying this the woman turning away, sighs,
And released a flood of tears
That overflowed her eye-lashes.

My face bowed, I, agitated,
Mumbling out the name in front of my woman.
Struck by fate, I began
To write something, embarrassed.
A series of lines emerged clearly,
Such that the end result somehow
Meant that very woman became utterly clear again
By her own bodily forms.

But then, recognizing it,
Her ruby-like cheeks sparkling,
The proud woman
Sobbing intensely,
"Oh! Her wondrous beauty!"
She proclaimed, tears turbid,
And stamped her foot angrily—
A veritable Brahma weapon—on my head.

«Kaṭhina|hṛdaye!
muñca bhrāntiṃ vyalīka|kath"|āśritāṃ!
Piśuna|vacanair
duḥkhaṃ netuṃ na yuktam imaṃ janam.
kim idam athavā
satyaṃ, mugdhe, tvay" âdya viniścitam?
Yad abhirucitaṃ,
tan me kṛtvā, priye, sukham āsyatām!»

Rātrau vāribhir ālas'|âmbuda|rav'|
ôdvignena jāt'|âśruṇā
pānthen' ātma|viyoga|duḥkha|piśunaṃ
gītaṃ tath" ôtkaṇṭhayā,
āstāṃ jīvita|hāriṇaḥ pravasan'|
ālāpasya saṃkīrtanaṃ,
mānasy' âpi jal'|âñjaliḥ sarabhasaṃ
lokena datto yathā.

55 Svaṃ dṛṣṭvā karaja|kṣataṃ, madhu|mada|
kṣīb", âvicāry' ērṣyayā
gacchantī, «kva nu gacchas' îti?» vidhṛtā
bālā paṭ'|ânte mayā.
pratyāvṛtta|mukhī, sabāṣpa|nayanā,
«māṃ muñca! muñc' êti!» sā
kopa|prasphurit'|âdharā yad avadat,
tat kena vismāryate?

"Callous woman! Let go of these slanderous suspicions.
It is not right
To bring misery to this man
With vicious words.
Or is this the truth
You have decided upon, delicate woman?
Do whatever you like to me.
Be happy!"

A tearful traveler in the night,
Agitated by rumbling clouds lazy with water,
Conveyed so anxiously
The distress in separation from his lover
That the people eagerly gave
An offering to wounded pride
And prohibited any mention
Of talk of travelling as it dampens life.

When she saw her own scratches on my hand, 55
Drunk with wine, unthinking, jealously leaving,
"Why are you going," I say
And seized the young girl on her sari's edge.
Face turned around, eyes tearful,
"Release me! Release me!"
Her lower lip throbbed angrily.
Who could forget anything she said?

Capala|hṛdaye!
  kiṃ svātantryāt tathā gṛham āgataḥ,
caraṇa|patitaḥ,
  prem'|ārdr'|ārdraḥ priyaḥ samupekṣitaḥ?
Tad idam adhunā
  yāvaj|jīvaṃ nirasta|sukh'|ôdayā,
rudita|śaraṇā,
  durjātānāṃ sahasva ruṣāṃ phalam!

«Bāle!» «nātha!» «vimuñca, mānini, ruṣaṃ!»
  «roṣān mayā kiṃ kṛtam?»
«khedo 'smāsu.» «na me 'parādhyati bhavān.
  sarve 'parādhā mayi.»
«tat kiṃ rodiṣi gadgadena vacasā?»
  «kasy' âgrato rudyate?»
«nanv etan mama?» «kā tav' âsmi?» «dayitā!»
  «n' âsm' îty! ato rudyate.»

«Śliṣṭaḥ kaṇṭhe kim iti na mayā
  mūḍhayā prāṇa|nāthaḥ?
cumbaty asmin vadana|vinatiḥ
  kiṃ kṛtā? kiṃ na dṛṣṭaḥ?
n' ôktaḥ kasmād iti?» nava|vadhū|
  ceṣṭitaṃ cintayantī,
paścāt|tāpaṃ vahati taruṇī,
  premṇi jāte rasajñā.

Fickle-hearted woman!
At his own behest he came home
Bowed at your feet and utterly overflowed with love.
Why have you rejected your lover?
Now for as long as life will last, any happiness is finished,
Weeping will be your refuge.
Suffer the lot of those who are wretched with anger.

"Young girl!"
"Lord!"
"Let go of your anger, proud woman!"
"What matters anger to me?"
"It troubles me."
"You have done no wrong to me.
All the wrongs are on me."
"Then why are you sobbing so?"
"In front of whom do I weep?"
"Isn't it me?"
"What am I to you?"
"Loved!"
"I am not! So I weep."

"When still innocent,
I did not embrace the Lord of my life's neck. Why?
When he kissed me, I bowed my face. Why?
I did not look at him. Why?"
Worrying about a new wife's behavior
The young woman then carries her regrets,
Knowing its tastes when love has arisen.

Śrutvā nām' âpi yasya
sphuṭa|ghana|pulakaṃ jāyate 'ṅgaṃ samantāt;
dṛṣṭvā yasy' ānan'|ênduṃ
bhavati vapur idaṃ candra|kānt'|ânukāri;
tasminn āgatya kaṇṭha|
graha|nikaṭa|pada|sthāyini prāṇa|nāthe,
bhagnā mānasya cintā,
bhavati mayi punar vajramayyāṃ kadā cit.

60 Lākṣā|lakṣma|lalāṭa|paṭṭam abhitaḥ,
keyūra|mudrā gale,
vaktre kajjala|kālimā nayanayos,
tāmbūla|rāgo 'paraḥ.
dṛṣṭvā kopa|vidhāyi maṇḍanam idaṃ
prātaś ciraṃ preyaso,
līlā|tāmaras'|ôdare mṛga|dṛśaḥ
śvāsāḥ samāptiṃ gatāḥ.

Lolair locana|vāribhiḥ saśapathaiḥ
pāda|praṇāmaiḥ priyaiḥ
anyās tā vinivārayanti kṛpaṇāḥ
Prāṇ'|ēśvaraṃ prasthitam.
puṇy'|âhaṃ, vraja, maṅgalaṃ sudivasaṃ.
prātaḥ prayātasya te
yat sneh'|ôcitam īhitaṃ, priya, mayā,
tan nirgataḥ śroṣyasi.

On merely hearing his name
My entire body palpably thrills.
On seeing his moon-like face
My body becomes like moon-stone.
On the Lord of my life returning,
Close enough to embrace me,
Prideful anxiety is broken
In me, yet again, adamantine as ever.

Red marks on his forehead, 60
Arm bracelet imprinted on his neck,
Black collyrium on his face,
Red betel stain on his eyes.
Long in the morning
Did the doe-eyed woman gaze
At her lover's outrageous ornament,
And her heavy sighs
Die in a lotus twiddling in her hand.

By their rolling, tearful eyes, promises
Draping themselves at men's feet and pleasantries,
These other pitiable women
Prevent the Lord of life departing.
This day is auspicious, bright.
Go at dawn and, once departed,
What is deemed appropriate for our love, dear man,
That you will hear, once you have left.

Lagnā n' âṅśuka|pallave, bhuja|latā
 na dvāra|deśe 'rpitā,
no vā pāda|yuge svayaṃ nipatitaṃ,
 «tiṣṭh' êti!» n' ôktaṃ vacaḥ.
kāle kevalam ambud'|āli|maline
 gantuṃ pravṛttaḥ śaṭhas
tanvyā bāṣpa|jal'|âugha|kalpita|nadī|
 pūreṇa ruddhaḥ priyaḥ.

Āstāṃ viśvasanaṃ sakhīṣu, vidit'|
 âbhiprāya|sāre jane
tatr' âpy arpayituṃ dṛśaṃ suracitāṃ
 śaknomi na vrīḍayā.
loko 'py eṣa par'|ôpahāsa|caturaḥ
 sūkṣm'|êṅgita|jño 'py alaṃ.
mātaḥ, kaṃ śaraṇaṃ vrajāmi? hṛdaye
 jīrṇo 'nurāg'|ânalaḥ.

Na jāne, saṃmukhāyate
 priyāṇi vadati priye,
sarvāṇy aṅgāni kiṃ yānti
 netratāṃ kim u karṇatām?

65 Analpa|cintā|bhara|moha|niścalā,
 vilokyamān" âiva karoti sādhvasam
svabhāva|śobh"|ānati|mātra|bhūṣaṇā,
 tanus tav' êyaṃ bata kiṃ nu, sundari?

Clung not to the edge of his garment,
Slender arm not thrown across the doorstop,
Thrown herself not at his feet
Nor said she, "Stay!"
At that very time, sky stained by clouds,
The rogue ready to leave,
The slender woman stops her lover
With a virtual river of tears.

Trust in my friends is suspended.
And on that man—he knows perfectly
    all my intentions—
I cannot cast a well contrived glance,
Too embarrassed am I.
The people too are skilled in the ridicule of others,
Skilled in reading subtle hints.
Mother, to which man can I go for refuge?
Passion's fire has withered in my heart.

I don't know.
When my approaching lover says lovely things
Have all my limbs
Become eyes or ears?

"Bewildered—holding such a weight of anxiety, 65
    you stay motionless,
Merely looking around—you evoke alarm.
Your mere bow an ornament— splendor itself.
Why so slender, beautiful woman?"

Iti priye pṛcchati, māna|vihvalā
  kathaṃcid antar|dhṛta|bāṣpa|gadgadam,
«na kiṃcid ity» eva jagāda yad vadhūḥ.
  kiyan na ten' âiva tay" âsya varṇitam.

Viraha|viṣamaḥ
  Kāmo vāmas tanū|kurute tanum.
divasa|gaṇanā|
  dakṣaś c' âyaṃ vyapeta|ghṛṇo Yamaḥ.
tvam api vaśago
  māna|vyādher. vicintaya, Nātha he!
kisalaya|mṛdur
  jīved evaṃ kathaṃ pramadā|janah?

«Pād'|āsakte suciram iha te
  vāmatā k" âiva mugdhe?
mand'|ārambhe praṇiyini jane
  ko 'parādh'|ôparodhaḥ?»
itthaṃ tasyāḥ parijana|kathā|
  komale kopa|vege,
bāṣp'|ôdbhedais tad anu sahasā
  na sthitaṃ na pravṛttam.

This her lover has asked, but agitated by wounded pride,
Tears held inside, somehow
The young wife just stammered, "Nothing."
Too much rests on him for her to describe.

The god of love—under the strain of separation
—charms,
Makes the body thin.
With skill in reckoning the days,
Devoid of compassion—Death.
Even you are subservient
To the disease of pride, Lord. Think:
Could a woman—wanton—soft as a bud
Live like this?

"Your artless lover stays attached long to your feet.
So why your disfavor?
Your lover is so slow to act,
So why trouble yourself over any betrayal?"
When the impetuosity of her anger softens
Following her friends' words,
Her welling tears could neither be stopped
Nor could they proceed.

Tath" âbhūd asmākaṃ
  prathamam avibhaktā tanur iyam.
tato na tvaṃ preyān,
  aham api hat'|āśā priyatamā.
idānīṃ nāthas tvaṃ,
  vayam api kalatraṃ. kim aparam?
may" āptaṃ prāṇānāṃ
  kuliśa|kaṭhinānāṃ phalam idam.

70 «Mugdhe! mugdhatay" âiva netum akhilaḥ
  kālaḥ kim ārabhyate?
mānaṃ dhatsva, dhṛtiṃ badhāna', rjutāṃ
  dūre kuru preyasi!»
sakhy" âivaṃ pratibodhitā, prativacas
  tām āha bhīt'|ānanā,
«Nīcaiḥ śaṃsa, hṛdi sthito hi nanu me
  Prāṇ'|ēśvaraḥ śroṣyati!»

«Kva prasthit" âsi, karabh'|ôru, ghane niśīthe?»
«prāṇ'|âdhiko vasati yatra janaḥ priyo me.»
«ekākinī bata kathaṃ na bibheṣi, bāle?»
«nanv asti puṅkhita|śaro Madanaḥ sahāyaḥ.»

This is how it was.
At first we were inseparable.
Then you were not my lover.
Despairing, I still loved you.
Now you are husband
And I wife. What else is there?
For people hard as diamond
This is all I've got.

"Delicate woman! Why allow all your time 70
To be passed in naïve expectancy?
Retain your angry pride! Bind your resolve!
Do not be open toward your lover."
Admonished such by her friend,
Timid, she responded,
"Speak softly. The Lord of my life
Stands in my heart! He might hear."

"Woman of abundant thighs
To where have you departed in the deep of night?"
"Where my beloved man is,
He who is dearer than life."
"Beware, young girl. Utterly alone,
Are you not afraid?"
"But don't I have Kama, with his arrows
As my companion?"

Līlā|tāmaras'|āhato, 'nya|vanitā|
niḥśaṅka|daṣṭ'|âdharaḥ,
kaś cit kesara|dūṣit'|ēkṣana iva
vyāmīlya netre sthitaḥ.
mugdhā kuḍmalit'|ānan'|êndu, dadatī
vāyuṃ, sthitā tatra sā,
bhrāntyā dhūrtatay" âthavā natim ṛte
ten' âniśaṃ cumbitā.

«Sphuṭatu hṛdayaṃ,
Kāmaḥ kāmaṃ karotu tanuṃ tanum.
na, sakhi, capala|
premṇā kāryaṃ punar dayitena me.»
iti sarabhasaṃ
mān'|āveśād udīrya vacas tayā,
ramaṇa|padavī
sāraṅg'|âkṣyā nirantaram īkṣitā.

«Gāḍh'|āśleṣa|viśīrṇa|candana|rajaḥ|
puñja|prakarṣād iyaṃ
śayyā saṃprati, komal'|âṅgi, paruṣ" êty,»
āropya māṃ vakṣasi,
gāḍh'|âuṣṭha|graha|pūrvam, ākulatayā,
pād'|âgra|saṃdaṃśaken'
ākṛṣy' âmbaram, ātmano yad ucitaṃ,
dhūrtena tat prastutam.

Bitten fearlessly on the lip by another woman,
He—now struck by an ornamental lotus—
Closed his eyes continually,
As if irritated by the filament of a lotus.
She—the delicate young girl, moonlight face puckered,
Stood there, blowing air,
Whether from mistake or cunning.
Without bowing he kissed her constantly.

"Let my heart burst!
Let Kama willingly make my body thin.
Friend, of what use do I have
For this lover, so transient in love?"
Passionately spoken,
In consequence of her domination by angry pride,
The doe-eyed woman gazed ceaselessly
Toward her lover's path.

"Such a mass of sandalwood dust
Scattered about by our tight embrace.
It has made this bed coarse, tender woman!"
And so he placed me on his chest,
Bit my lip in his arousal
Dragged off my sari
The tips of his toes acting as pincers.
The scoundrel did whatever suited him.

75 Katham api kṛta|
pratyākhyāne priye skhalit'|ôttare,
viraha|kṛśayā
kṛtvā vyājaṃ prakalpitam aśrutam.
asahana|sakhī|
śrotra|prāpti|pramāda|sasaṃbhramam,
vigalita|dṛśā
śūnye gehe samucchvasitaṃ punaḥ.

Ā|dṛṣṭi|prasarāt priyasya padavīm
udvīkṣya, nirviṇṇayā
vicchinneṣu pathiṣv, ahaḥ|pariṇatau,
dhvānte samutsarpati,
dattv" âikaṃ saśucā gṛhaṃ prati padaṃ,
pānthaḥ striy" âsmin kṣaṇe,
mā bhūd āgata ity, amanda|valita|
grīvaṃ punar vīkṣitam.

Āyāte dayite, manoratha|śatair
nītvā kathaṃ cid dinam,
vaidagdhy'|âpagamāj jaḍe parijane
dīrghāṃ kathāṃ kurvati,
«daṣṭ" âsm' îty!» abhidhāya satvara|padaṃ
vyādhūya cīn'|âṃśukam,
tanv|aṅgyā rati|kātareṇa manasā
nītaḥ pradīpaḥ śamam.

When the rejected lover 75
Somehow responds in halting voice,
Thin through separation, the woman
Took a stance, contrived not to hear.
Flustered by her carelessness, what he said
had reached a jealous friend's ear.
Her eyes dry, she once again breathed easily.
The house was empty.

A despondent wife scanned
Her husband's path to her vision's limit,
Now few travelers grace the road, day is ended,
Darkness glides in.
She placed one foot toward the house
At which very moment the grieving traveller's wife
Thought he might have arrived,
Turned her head quickly, searched again.

Her lover had returned.
Somehow she passed the day with her hundred wishes.
Lacking any awareness
Her obtuse retinue extends their chatter.
"I have been bitten," she says,
Rapidly shaking her sari's edge,
And, desperate for love, the slender woman
Extinguished the lamp.

Ālamby' âṅgaṇā|vāṭikā|parisare
cūta|drume mañjarīṃ
sarpat|sāndra|parāga|lampaṭa|raṭad|
bhṛṅg'|âṅganā|śobhinīm,
manye, svāṃ tanum uttarīya|śakalen'
âcchādya bālā, sphurat|
kaṇṭha|dhvāna|nirodha|kampita|kuca|
śvās'|ôdgamā roditi.

«Yāsyām' îti» samudyatasya gaditaṃ
visrabdham ākarṇitaṃ.
gacchan dūram, upekṣito muhur asau
vyāvṛtya tiṣṭhann api.
tac chūnye punar āsthit" âsmi bhavane.
«prāṇās ta ete dṛḍhāḥ.
sakhyas, tiṣṭhata! jīvita|vyasaninī
dambhād ahaṃ rodimi.

80 Anālocya premṇaḥ
pariṇatim, anādṛtya suhṛdaḥ,
tvay" âkāṇḍe mānaḥ
kim iti, sarale, saṃprati kṛtaḥ?
samākṛṣṭā hy ete
pralaya|dahan'|ôdbhāsura|śikhāḥ
sva|hasten' âṅgārās.
tad alam adhun" âraṇya|ruditaiḥ.

From the tree near the women's garden
She picked mango blossoms
Splendid with *bhringa* bees and their mates
  gliding about,
Buzzing loudly, lusting for thick pollen.
I think, having concealed her body
With a piece of her upper garment,
That young girl sighs heavily, her agitated breasts
Stifling the sound in her pulsating throat,
As she weeps.

"I will go," he said, fully prepared.
I listened confidently.
Walking far he was ignored
Yet repeatedly turned around.
Once more, then, to an empty house I have returned.
"Living is hard.
Friends! Stay!
Addicted to life as I am, I falsely cry."

Without considering the outcome of your love, 80
Paying no respect to your friends,
Why have you now, restless woman,
Expressed your angry pride? The time is wrong.
By your own hand
You have collected the charcoals
—flames shining as in the cosmic destruction.
Now, stop weeping in a forest.

Kapole patrālī
  kara|tala|nirodhena mṛditā.
nipīto niḥśvāsair
  ayam amṛta|hṛdyo 'dhara|rasaḥ.
muhuḥ kaṇṭhe lagnas
  taralayati bāṣpaḥ stana|taṭaṃ.
priyo manyur jātas
  tava, niranurodhe, na tu vayam.

Śūnyaṃ vāsa|gṛhaṃ vilokya, śayanād
  utthāya kiṃcic chanair,
nidrā|vyājam upāgatasya suciraṃ
  nirvarṇya patyur mukham,
visrabdhaṃ paricumbya, jāta|pulakām
  ālokya gaṇḍa|sthalīm,
lajjā|namra|mukhī priyeṇa hasatā
  bālā ciraṃ cumbitā.

Lolad|bhrū|latayā, vipakṣa|dig|u-
  panyāse 'vadhūtam śiraḥ.
Tad|vṛttānta|nirīkṣaṇe kṛta|namas|
  kāro vilakṣaḥ sthitaḥ.
Kopāt tāmra|kapola|bhittini mukhe
  dṛṣṭyā gataḥ pādayor.
Utsṛṣṭo guru|saṃnidhāv api vidhir
  dvābhyāṃ na kāl'|ôcitaḥ.

The streaked mascara on your cheek
Removed by your hand.
Your sighs dry up
Ambrosia-like nectar on your lips.
The clear forever stuck in your throat
Disturbs your breasts.
Anger has become your love, difficult woman,
Not I.

Seeing bedroom empty,
Getting up slowly from the bed,
Contemplating long the face
Of her husband, whose sleep was pretense,
Confidently covering his cheek with kisses,
Noticing his quivering skin,
That young girl, head bowed in embarrassment,
Was kissed long by her laughing lover.

The mere suggestion of her rival's house,
Her arched eyebrows twitching,
She shook her head.
On noticing her behavior
He made an act of obeisance and stood, perplexed.
His eyes fixed on her face, red cheeks angrily fissured,
He fell at her feet.
Even in front of their parents
These two did not eschew correct behavior.

Jātā n' ôtkalikā, stanau na lulitau,
gātraṃ na rom'|âñcitaṃ,
vaktraṃ sveda|kaṇ'|ânvitaṃ na sahasā,
yāvac chaṭhen' âmunā
dṛṣṭen' âiva mano hṛtaṃ, dhṛti|muṣā
Prāṇ'|ēśvareṇ' âdya me.
Tat ken' âtra nirūpyamāṇa|nipuṇo
mānaḥ samādhīyatām?

85 Dṛṣṭaḥ kātara|netrayā cirataraṃ,
baddh'|âñjaliṃ yācitaḥ,
paścād aṅśuka|pallavena vidhṛto,
nirvyājam āliṅgititaḥ,
ity ākṣipya yadā samastam aghṛṇo
gantuṃ pravṛttaḥ śaṭhaḥ,
pūrvaṃ prāṇa|patigraho dayitayā
muktas, tato vallabhaḥ.

Tapte mahā|viraha|vahni|śikh"|āvalībhir,
āpāṇḍura|stana|taṭe hṛdaye priyāyāḥ,
man|mārga|vīkṣaṇa|niveśita|dīna|dṛṣṭer
nūnaṃ chamac|cham iti bāṣpakaṇāḥ patanti.

Longing not arisen, breasts not tossed about,
Skin not quivered,
On my face no drops of sweat
Until suddenly—that scoundrel.
He has just appeared—the Lord of my life,
Plundered my fortitude, stole my heart.
How then should my angry pride be focussed,
So clever in its display?

He appeared. The woman of the timid eyes 85
Long requested a sign of greeting,
Held him by a strip of white cloth,
Embraced him openly.
When the cold-hearted rogue discarded all this
And prepared to go,
His lover renounced her desire for life,
Then for her lover.

Onto my beloved's heart,
Her pale sloping breasts,
Burned by rows of hot flames
—the fire of long separation—
Teardrops now fall,
Trickling down
From her sad eyes
Focussed on searching my path.

Cintā|moha|viniścalena manasā,
    maunena pāda'|ānataḥ
pratyākhyāna|parāṅmukhaḥ priyatamo
    gantuṃ pravṛtto 'dhunā.
savrīḍair, alasair, nirantara|luṭhad|
    bāṣp'|ākulair īkṣanaiḥ
śvās'|ôtkampi|kucaṃ nirīkṣya suciraṃ,
    jīv'|āśayā vāritaḥ.

Mlānaṃ, pāṇḍu, kṛśaṃ, viyoga|vidhuraṃ,
    lamb'|âlakaṃ, sālasam;
bhūyas tat|kṣaṇa|jāta|kānti rabhasa|
    prāpte mayi proṣite,
sāṭopaṃ, rati|kelik'|âlasa|rasaṃ,
    ramyaṃ kim apy ādarād,
yat pītaṃ sutanor mayā vadanakaṃ,
    vaktuṃ na tat pāryate.

«S" âiv' âhaṃ pramadā, nṛṇām adhigatāv
    etau ca tau nūpurau.
eṣ" âsmākam avṛttir eva; sahaja|
    vrīḍā|dhanaḥ strī|janaḥ.»
itthaṃ lajjitayā, smṛter upagame
    matvā tanuṃ saṃbhramāt,
puṃ|bhāvaḥ prathamaṃ rati|vyatikare
    muktas, tato vallabhaḥ.

Bowed at her feet, her lover,
Facing downwards, following her rejection
—silently, her mind petrified with uncertainty and
anxiety—
Was now ready to go.
But she, desirous of living,
Stopped him with tear-filled eyes
Trickling uninterrupted, languid and shy,
And after he had gazed long at her,
Whose breasts were heaving.

Faded, pale, drawn—depressed by my absence,
Curls dangling, listless.
Instantly her splendor returns
As soon as I return from my travels.
Proud, faintly languid from the play of sex,
So utterly lovely,
I carefully drink the slender woman's delicate face,
That I could not describe.

"I am certainly a mere wanton woman,
As these two anklets clearly said to men.
But this is certainly not our typical behavior.
A woman's wealth is her innate shyness."
By her accompanying shame, on recovering her wits
She hurriedly recognized her own body.
Firstly gave up sex in the man's position,
Then abandoned her lover.

90 Kara|kisalayaṃ
dhūtvā dhūtvā vimārgati vāsasī,
kṣipati sumano|
mālā|śeṣaṃ pradīpa|śikhāṃ prati,
sthagayati muhuḥ
patyur netre, vihasya samākulā,
surata|viratā
ramyā tanvī muhur muhur īkṣate.

Santy ev' âtra gṛhe gṛhe yuvatayas.
tāḥ pṛccha gatv" âdhunā:
preyāṅsaḥ praṇamanti kiṃ tava punar,
dāso yathā vartate.
ātma|drohiṇi, durjanaiḥ pralapitaṃ
karṇe 'niśaṃ mā kṛthāḥ.
chinna|sneha|rasā bhavanti puruṣā
duḥkh'|ânuvartyāḥ punaḥ.

Niḥśvāsā vadanaṃ dahanti, hṛdayaṃ
nirmūlam unmathyate,
nidrā n' aiti, na dṛśyate priya|mukhaṃ,
naktaṃ|divaṃ rudyate,
aṅgam śoṣam upaiti, pāda|patitaḥ
preyāns tath" ôpekṣitaḥ.
sakhyaḥ, kaṃ guṇam ākalayya dayite
mānaṃ vayaṃ kāritāḥ?

Moving her bud-like hand all about 90
She seeks her clothes,
Throws the rest of the flowers
Onto the lamp's flame.
Repeatedly concealing her husband's eyes,
Laughing, if flushed.
Lovemaking finished,
This lovely slender woman gazes constantly.

Young girls are in every house.
Go and ask them now
If their lovers bow
As yours, who is like a slave.
Self-pitying woman,
Never pay attention to malicious people's gossip.
Men who must constantly experience misery
Are liable to lose their taste for love.

Sighs burning my face,
Whole heart churning,
Sleep goes, lover's face disappears,
Weeping day and night,
Body dries up.
My lover, bowed at my feet, I disregard.
Friends, what quality
Caused this angry pride toward my lover?

Ady' ārabhya yadi priye punar ahaṃ
mānasya v", ânyasya vā
gṛhṇīyām śaṭha|durnayena manasā
nām' âpi saṃkṣepataḥ,
tat ten' âiva vinā śaśāṅka|dhavalāḥ
spaṣṭ'|âṭṭahāsā niśā,
eko vā divasaḥ payoda|malino
yāyān mama prāvṛṣi.

«Idaṃ kṛṣṇaṃ.» «kṛṣṇaṃ.»
«priyatama, tanu śvetam.» «atha kim.»
«gamiṣyāmo.» «yāmo.»
«bhavatu gamanen'» «âtha bhavatu.»
purā yen' âivaṃ me
ciram anusṛtā citta|padavī,
sa ev' ânyo jātaḥ.
sakhi, paricitāḥ kasya puruṣāḥ?

95 Caraṇa|patanaṃ.
sakhy'|ālāpā. manohara|cāṭavaḥ.
kṛśatara|tanor
gāḍh'|āśleṣo. haṭhāt paricumbanam.
iti hi capalo
mān'|ārambhas, tath" âpi hi n' ôtsahe.
hṛdaya|dayitaḥ
kāntaḥ, kāmaṃ kim atra karomy aham.

From now on if
I express some minor word
of angry pride or something else against my lover
because of his villainous heart,
Then without him
For me the nights—dazzling moonlight—
Will be loud laughter,
A single day,
Will be stained with clouds as in the rainy season.

"It's black!" "It's black."
"Dearest, my body is white!"
"Definitely!"
"I will go."
"I am going."
"It will certainly be by this path."
"Yes."
"He—once pursued lengthily
The pathway of my heart—
Has now become someone else, friend.
Who can understand a man?"

Prostration. Gossip. Captivating flattery. 95
Fiercely embracing my slender body.
Passionate kissing.
This expression of angry pride is erratic.
But I can't stand it.
I cherish my husband.
What can I do?

Tanv|aṅgyā guru|saṃnidhau nayanayor
yad vāri saṃstambhitaṃ,
ten' ântargalitena manmatha|śikhī
sikto viyog'|ôdbhavaḥ.
manye, tasya nirasyamāna|kiraṇasy'
âiṣā mukhen' ôdgatā
śvās'|āyāsa|samākul'|âli|saraṇi|
vyājena dhūm'|āvalī.

Bhrū|bhedo guṇitaś ciraṃ, nayanayor
abhyastam āmīlanaṃ,
roddhum śikṣitam ādareṇa hasitaṃ,
maune 'bhiyogaḥ kṛtaḥ,
dhairyaṃ kartum api sthirīkṛtam idaṃ
cetaḥ kathaṃcin mayā.
baddho māna|parigrahe parikaraḥ,
siddhis tu daive sthitā.

Ahaṃ ten' āhūtā,
«kim api kathayām' îti» vijane.
samīpe c' āsīnā,
sarasa|hṛdayatvād avahitā.
tataḥ karṇ'|ôpānte
kimapi vadat" āghrāya vadanam,
gṛhītā dhammille,
sakhi, sa ca mayā gāḍham adhare.

In front of her parents
The slender woman stopped her tears,
Which flowed within,
Sprinkled love's flame, sprung forth through
    separation.
Extinguishing this flame
Her mouth pushes up a wreath of smoke
—a line of bees confused by her anxious sighing,
It seems.

Frowned long and intensely,
Practiced closing my eyes,
Carefully learned not to laugh,
Applied the art of silence
—To effect composure—
Somehow steeled my heart.
Much have I prepared to express my pride.
Its success depends on fate.

"I will tell you something."
So summoned was I to a private spot.
Close I sat,
Attentive, my longing heart.
Then, whispering it in my ear,
Kissing my mouth,
He seized the braid of my hair friend,
And I seized him tightly on the lip.

Deśair antaritā, śataiś ca saritām,
urvī|bhṛtāṃ kānanair.
yatnen' âpi na yāti locana|pathaṃ
kānt", êti jānann api
udgrīvaś, caraṇ'|ârdha|ruddha|vasudhaḥ,
pronmṛjya sāsre dṛśau,
tām āśāṃ pathikas tath" âpi kim api
dhyāyan punar vīkṣate.

100 Cakṣuḥ|prīti|prasakte
manasi, paricaye cintyamān'|âbhyupāye,
rāge yāte 'tibhūmiṃ,
vikasati sutarāṃ gocare dūtikāyāḥ,
āstāṃ dūreṇa tāvat
sarabhasa|dayit"|āliṅgan'|ānanda|lābhas,
tad|geh'|ôpānta|rathyā|
bhramaṇam api parāṃ nirvṛtiṃ saṃtanoti.

Kānte talpam upāgate vigalitā
nīvī svayaṃ bandhanād,
vāso viślatha|mekhalā|guṇa|dhṛtaṃ
kiṃ cin nitambe sthitam.
etāvat, sakhi, vedmi sāṃpratam ahaṃ.
tasy' âṅga|saṅge punar
«ko 'yaṃ?» «k" âsmi?» «rataṃ nu vā katham iti?»
svalp" âpi me na smṛtiḥ.

She—separated by entire lands
Hundreds of rivers and mountain-clad forests.
That lovely woman—try as he might
He cannot see.
He knows this, yet neck upraised, on tiptoe,
Wiping teary eyes,
The traveler looked constantly at her direction,
Lost in thought.

When the mind is rapt merely by a sight 100
And a plan for a meeting considered,
And passion becomes intense,
And the scope for the messenger increases still more
Leaving aside
The bliss of the lover's embrace,
Even wandering the road near her house
Extends to a man the highest bliss.

My husband approached the bed,
My sari's knot untied itself,
My sari, held by slackened girdle,
Somehow just rested on my hips.
I know that much now, friend!
But once again locked in his embrace,
"Who is he?" "Who am I?" "Is this lovemaking?"
Of this I have not the slightest recollection.

Prāsāde sā, diśi diśi ca sā,
  pṛṣṭhataḥ sā, puraḥ sā,
paryaṅke sā, pathi pathi ca sā
  tad|viyog'|āturasya.
haṃhaś cetaḥ! prakṛtir aparā
  n' âsti me k" âpi. sā, sā,
sā, sā, sā, sā jagati sakale.
  ko 'yam advaita|vādaḥ?

To the man anguished in separation,
On the terrace is she, everywhere is she,
Behind is she, in front is she,
On the couch is she, on the path is she.
Behold! Heart! No woman is better
To me. She, she,
She, she, she, she
In this entire world.
What's this talk of unity?

THE FIFTY STANZAS OF A THIEF

The Fifty Stanzas of a Thief (Sanskrit: *Caura/pañcā-śikā*) are traditionally attributed to Bílhana, who was active in the second half of the eleventh century CE. A Kashmiri brahmin, he travelled to various Indian courts, and probably settled in Kalyána (in modern Hyderabad), where he wrote a long historical poem celebrating his patron the Chálukya king Vikramáditya VI Tri·bhúvana·malla (1076–1127).

The Thief has stolen the affections of a princess, and the poem in detached stanzas describes their clandestine love. Evidently extrapolated from the poem itself (especially stanzas 31, 28, 49, 27) is the legend surrounding its composition: the poet had fallen in love with the daughter of a royal patron; when her pregnancy was noticed he was caught, imprisoned, and condemned to death; but as he was led to execution in the king's presence he recited these reminiscences of his happier days, and the king was so moved that he ordered his release and formally gave him his daughter in marriage.

The poem is a straightforward and unelaborate example of a major genre of Sanskrit literature called *kāvya*. *Kāvya* corresponds precisely to no English term; but the one-word English translation is poetry. *Kāvya* like poetry is usually in verse but not coextensive with verse: not all verse is *kāvya* nor is all *kāvya* in verse. The ancient Indians were prolific in theories of poetics and hence in definitions of *kāvya* but perhaps the commonest definition is in terms of a quality called *rasa*. This word is a metaphor from tasting, and means "flavor." The English word used in corresponding context is probably "atmosphere," and the nearest approximation within our tradition is "mode," but both these lack the correct connotations, and I shall go on using "flavor." *Kāvya* then, or poetry, is any coherent speech or writing which is informed by flavor.

A flavor is an emotion or sentiment, not experienced directly as in real life, but aesthetically, so that it affords a calm enjoyment, a dispassionate pleasure in the passions. This aesthetic transfiguration is described as the "universalization" of our passions so that we experience them without being involved in a real situation: a man who sees two lovers in real life, it was said, might undergo emotions of lust, repulsion, or envy; but in reacting to a work of art he experiences their passion as the type of his own experience of love. There are usually held to be eight basic flavors: love, mirth, grief, anger, heroism, fear, loathing, amazement. Some of these are subdivided; our poem has both the subdivided flavors "love in separation" and "love in enjoyment." Each work of literature will theoretically have one flavor dominant throughout; and there are rules stating which ancillary flavors may be used in a work dominated by each particular flavour without disrupting the total effect. The word *rasa* is used in a conceit at the end of stanza 24, and I owe the ingenious translation to MICHAEL COULSON.

Poetic theory also recognizes the use of "ornaments," corresponding to our "figures"; ornaments can be of sense or of sound, and include simile, metaphor, zeugma, etc. In early theory *rasa* was merely one such ornament. According to another theory, which came to be held in conjunction with the *rasa* theory, true *kāvya* is literature in which that meaning which is suggested, not directly expressed, is the more important.

I made this translation while studying Sanskrit literature under Professor DANIEL INGALLS at Harvard in 1962–3, when there were hardly any readable translations of *kāvya* in print. At that time INGALLS was putting the finishing touches to his monumental work of translation and exposition, *An Anthology of Sanskrit Court Poetry* which came out in 1965. INGALLS' introductory essay "Sanskrit Poetry and Sankrit Poetics" (pp. 2–29) makes it unnecessary for me to say more on this topic.

Unfortunately no authoritative text of this poem exists, and I have had to edit my own. The poem has been published in three main recensions, but between these the choice was simple, for only one has just the fifty stanzas of the title, and these all beginning with the same word, plainly an original feature. However, even of this recension not all editions have the same fifty stanzas. Forty-eight of my stanzas are from one text which seemed to me the best; I have emended it where necessary. My stanzas 12 and 40 are from another text. The stanza 40 in the best text is corrupt beyond intelligibility or redemption; stanza 44 is hardly better; but my translation, numbered 44, combines all intelligible content from both main extant versions. My stanza 12 is introduced for another reason: stanzas 12 and 13 of the best text are so empty and repetitious, partly of notions difficult to render tasteful to a modern reader that I have combined them in my stanza 13. This is the only place where I have allowed myself such a liberty, though even here I have omitted no idea which is in the Sanskrit. Otherwise this translation is literal: it contains virtually every word of the original, and adds almost nothing, though I have on occasion over-translated what in Sanskrit has become a *cliché*, in order not to forfeit the exoticism of a foreign culture.

The original Sanskrit is in four-line stanzas, each line having fourteen syllables. My stanzas of six iambic pentameters are thus almost the same length as the Sanskrit. All Sanskrit metres are quantitative and most are composed of a fixed pattern of long and short syllables without division into feet. (In recitation the voice dwells on the long syllables.) This poem is in a common lyric metre called *vasanta/tilakā* which means "Ornament of spring," it scans -- ⏑- ⏑⏑⏑- ⏑⏑- ⏑--, four times. Like other metres of its type it has no alternative forms (though the last syllable of each line is common, as in all Indo-European metres).

I have attempted to convey something of this formal strictness by adopting a rather exacting rhyming scheme and rigid metre. In this I differ from my colleagues, especially my American colleagues. Partly it is a question of national and individual taste. In translating Sanskrit, the "elaborated" language, I do not think it necessary to eschew poetic diction. The difference is also one of material: this is a poem which depends hardly at all on punning, alliteration, or other "ornaments of sound," and little on suggestions which might elude a non-Indianist. This has allowed me to try to make an impression on the readers of this translation at least analogous to the impression made on its Indian audience by the recitation of the Sanskrit. I hope that my translation, which is likewise designed to be read aloud, portrays both the matter and the manner of the original as nearly as may be.

Most of the allusions which need explanation are mythological. The Indian god of love (1, 2, 20, 29, 32, 42), equivalent in function to Cupid, is called Kama, which means passion or sexual love; any synonym can also be used as his name. He shoots people with flower arrows (20) which inflict the fire of love (2, 42); he is married to Rati (Pleasure) (29,32). The trinity of gods mentioned in 30 are Brahma, Vishnu and Shiva. They bear no resemblance or relation to the Christian Trinity; any one of then can be seen as supreme. Brahma is the Creator in 39. Vishnu had several incarnations; one was as a tortoise (50); the most famous was as Krishna. His wife Lakshmi or Shri (both words mean "good Fortune") (3, 39) is also the goddess of beauty, and was born at the churning of the ocean (see below); at birth she either held a lotus in her hand or floated on the expanded petals of a lotus. Shiva (39,50) (the name means "kindly" and is euphemistic) is married to Párvati (39), daughter of Mt. Himálaya. His wild *tāṇḍava* dance, which he dances at the periodic dissolution of the world, is compared in 7 to the motions of love-making. Indra (39) was in very ancient times an extremely important god, but later became merely the god of sky and storm, ruler over a heaven populated by comparatively lowly gods.

Though these gods never experience old age (27), Indians consider their condition inferior to liberation from the cycle of re-birth. Stanzas 27, 33, 41 and 42 suggest the doctrine that one's last living thought determines one's fate after death.

I hope the complex allusion of 50 is tolerably clear in my translation. The story is that the gods churned the ocean for the nectar of immortality within it. They used Mt. Mándara as their churning stick and a giant serpent as the rope; Vishnu as a tortoise made his back the pivot. Thirteen treasures, including Lakshmi, wine, and the moon, came out of the ocean, but so did a deadly poison which would have destroyed the world had not Shiva drunk it, thus staining his throat blue. The ocean prevented the equally dangerous submarine fire from emerging. Incidentally, Ocean's retention of the submarine fire is also alluded to in the last verse of the eighth canto of Kali·dasa's great poem the *Kumāra/sambhava* and its occurence in the last verse of our poem sounds to me like an echo, which would support the traditional view that the eighth is the last canto which is really by Kali·dasa.

A few Sanskrit literary conventions about nature also require explanation. The *Michelia campaka* (1) is a tree with a fragrant yellow flower. The *aśoka* tree (14) *(Saraca indica)* is said to bloom when touched by the foot of a beautiful woman; this makes the metaphor doubly apt. I hope other conceits common in Sanskrit poetry can be understood from the translation; for example, in stanza 2 he shivers because the rays of the moon are cold as the sun's are hot. Moonbeams are the alleged diet of the *cakora* bird (12), a kind of partridge *(Perdix rufa)*.

NOTES

1 Harvard Oriental Series vol. 44, Cambridge, Mass. 1965.

Ady' âpi tāṃ kanaka|campaka|dāma|gaurīṃ
phull'|âravinda|vadanāṃ tanu|roma|rājīm
supt'|ôtthitāṃ madana|vihvala|s'|alas'|âṅgīṃ
vidyāṃ pramāda|galitām iva cintayāmi

Ady' âpi tāṃ śaśi|mukhīṃ nava|yauvan'|āḍhyāṃ
pīna|stanīṃ punar ahaṃ yadi gaura|kāntim
paśyāmi manmatha|śar'|ânala|pīḍit'|âṅgīṃ
gātrāṇi saṃprati karomi su|śītalāni

Ady' âpi tāṃ yadi punaḥ kamal'|āyat'|âkṣīṃ
paśyāmi pīvara|payodhara|bhāra|khinnām
saṃpīḍya bāhu|yugalena pibāmi vaktram
unmattavan madhukaraḥ kamalaṃ yath" êṣṭam

Ady' âpi tāṃ nidhuvana|klama|niḥ|sah'|âṅgīm
ā|pāṇḍu|gaṇḍa|patit'|âlaka|kuntal'|ālim
pracchanna|pāpa|kṛta|mantharam āvahantīṃ
kaṇṭh'|âvasakta|mṛdu|bāhu|latāṃ smarāmi

Still I recall her, golden as a wreath
Of *chámpaka* flowers, her full-blown lotus face,
Her slender line of down, her limbs confused
By Passion, faint from passionate embrace;
I recollect her as she rose from sleep
Like knowledge carelessness has failed to keep.

Still when I see the richness of her youth,
The moon her face, the swelling of her breast.
Her beauty's pallor, and her every limb
By Kama's fire-bearing darts distressed,
Even today as I recall that sight
My limbs grow cold and shiver with delight.

Still when her eyes, as lotus petals long,
Like Fortune's, goddess lotus-born, I see,
And see her wearied by her bosom's load,
With both my arms clasping her close to me
As honey-bee his darling lotus sips
I would grow drunk on mead within her lips.

Still I remember how her body lay
Exhausted by our love, her pale cheeks lined
With tumbled locks of hair, and round my neck
The tendrils of her arms she tightly twined;
Held me so close as if she bore within
Her heart concealed some secret deed of sin.

5 Ady' âpi tāṃ surata|jāgara|ghūrṇamāna|
tiryag|valat|tarala|tāraka|dīrgha|netrām
śṛṅgāra|sāra|kamal'|ākara|rāja|haṃsīṃ
vrīḍā|vinamra|vadanām uṣasi smarāmi

Ady' âpi tāṃ yadi punaḥ śravaṇ'|āyat'|âkṣīṃ
paśyāmi dīrgha|viraha|jvarit'|âṅga|yaṣṭim
aṅgair ahaṃ samupaguhya tato 'tigāḍhaṃ
n' ônmīlayāmi nayane na ca tāṃ tyajāmi

Ady' âpi tāṃ surata|tāṇḍava|sūtra|dhārīṃ
pūrṇ'|êndu|sundara|mukhīṃ mada|vihval'|âṅgīm
tanvīṃ viśāla|jaghana|stana|bhāra|namrāṃ
vyālola|kuntala|kalāpavatīṃ smarāmi

Ady' âpi tāṃ masṛṇa|candana|paṅka|miśra|
kastūrikā|parimal'|ôttha|visarpi|gandhām
anyonya|cañcu|puṭa|cumbana|khañjarīṭa|
yugm'|âbhirāma|nayanāṃ śayane smarāmi

Still I remember sleepless nights we passed
In pleasure; her long eyes at break of day,
Tremulous roving stars, threw sidelong looks
Towards me, as in shame she turned away.
A swan princess into a lotus bed
Upon a lake of love inclined her head.

Still, could I once again behold my love,
Her eyes so long they seemed to touch her ears,
Could I behold my darling's slender form,
Long racked by parted lovers' tender fears,
I'd clasp that body wasted by love's fever
And close my eyes, and never more would leave her.

Still I recall that lovely full-moon face,
The disarray of her dishevelled tresses,
The weight of ample hips and bosom, which
Her dainty, passion-weary limbs depresses;
These attributes her leading role enhance
In love's ecstatic, earth-dissolving dance.

Still I recall the grace of her repose
As she reclined, with perfume all around
Arising from the fragrant musk of deer
Blended with smoothest sandal finely ground.
Her eyes in lovely fluttering imitate
A curve-beaked wagtail billing with his mate.

Ady' âpi tāṃ nidhuvane madhu|pāna|raktāṃ
līl"|âdharāṃ kṛśa|tanuṃ capal'|āyat'|âkṣīm
kāśmīra|paṅka|mṛga|nābhi|kṛt'|âṅga|rāgāṃ
karpūra|pūga|paripūrṇa|mukhīṃ smarāmi

10 Ady' âpi tat kanaka|gaura|kṛt'|âṅga|rāgaṃ
prasveda|bindu|vitataṃ vadanaṃ priyāyāḥ
ante smarāmi rati|kheda|vilola|netraṃ
Rāh'|ûparāga|parimuktam iv' êndu|bimbam

Ady' âpi tan manasi saṃparivartate me
rātrau mayi kṣutavati kṣiti|pāla|putryā
«jīv' êti!» maṅgala|vacaḥ parihṛtya kopāt
karṇe kṛtaṃ kanaka|patram anālapantyā

Ady' âpi tāṃ cala|cakora|vilola|netrāṃ
śīt'|âṃśu|maṇḍala|mukhīṃ kuṭil'|âgra|keśām
matt'|êbha|kumbha|sadṛśa|stana|bhāra|namrāṃ
bandhūka|puṣpa|sadṛś'|áuṣṭha|puṭāṃ smarāmi.

Still I recall her flushed with love and wine,
Great eyes in which the darting pupils swim,
Her slender body and her sportive lips;
On a ground of Kashmir saffron every limb
With figures in black deer-musk ornamented;
Her mouth with camphor and with betel scented.

Still I remember my beloved's face
Gleaming with pearls of sweat and saffron's gold;
The abundant moisture and her wandering eyes
All the fatigue of love's fulfillment told.
No brighter does the full-faced moon appear
When from Eclipse's jaws she frees her sphere.

Still I remember how one night, offended,
The princess would not speak, and so refrained
When I had sneezed from the auspicious words
"Long life!," by which such omens are restrained,
But wordlessly upon her ear reset
The golden leaf which was her amulet.

Still I remember, ringed with curls, her face,
A rotund moon on whose cool rays were fed
Two swift *chakóra* birds, her restless eyes;
Her lips as the *bandhúka* bloom were red;
She bowed with heavy breasts as prominent
As temples of a rutting elephant.

Ady’ âpi tat|praṇaya|bhaṅgura|dṛṣṭi|pātaṃ
tasyāḥ smarāmi rati|vibhrama|gātra|bhaṅgam
vastr’|âñcala|skhalata|cāru|payodhar’|ântaṃ
danta|cchadaṃ daśana|khaṇḍana|maṇḍanaṃ ca

Ady’ âpy aśoka|nava|pallava|rakta|hastāṃ
muktā|phala|pracaya|cumbita|cūcuk’|âgrām
antaḥ smit’|ôcchvasita|pāṇḍura|gaṇḍa|bhittiṃ
tāṃ vallabhām alasa|haṃsa|gatiṃ smarāmi.

Ady’ âpi tat|kanaka|reṇu|ghan’|ōru|deśe
nyastaṃ smarāmi nakhara|kṣata|lakṣma tasyāḥ
ākṛṣṭa|hema|rucir’|âmbaram utthitāyā
lajjā|vaśāt kara|dhṛtaṃ ca tato vrajantyāḥ

Ady’ âpi tāṃ vidhṛta|kajjala|cāru|netrāṃ
protphulla|puṣpa|nikar’|ākula|keśa|pāśām
sindūra|saṃlulita|mauktika|hāra|dantām
ābaddha|hema|kaṭakāṃ rahasi smarāmi

*Still I recall the graceful coquetry
Of those curved limbs, the loving sidelong look,
The golden earrings beating on her cheeks
As sweat-pearl glistening her body shook.
Her slipping garment showed her lovely breast;
Her lip was dented where my teeth had pressed.

Still I recall my darling's hands, as red
As when the *ashóka* tree new buds unfurls.
Her gait was gentle, stately as a swan's;
Her nipples kissed by necklaces of pearls.
Her pallid cheeks my memory beguile:
They blossomed into dimples with her smile.

Still I recall the gold-anointed thigh
On which her gold-embroidered garment glinted.
As she got up I tugged it to reveal
The marks which my love-frenzied nails had printed.
Then in embarrassment she would not stay
But hid them with her hand and ran away.

Still I remember when I am alone
The jet-black eyes collyrium had kissed;
Her braided hair, one mass of full-blown flowers;
And golden bangles dangling from each wrist.
Sweet betel-juice had tinged her teeth with red—
A string of pearls smeared with vermilion lead.

Ady' âpi tāṃ galita|bandhana|keśa|pāśāṃ
srasta|srajaṃ smita|sudhā|madhur'|âdhar'|âuṣṭhīm
pīn'|ônnata|stana|yug'|ôpavicāra|cumban|
mukt'|āvalīṃ rahasi lola|dṛśam smarāmi

Ady' âpi tāṃ dhavala|veśmani ratna|dīpa|
mālā|mayūkha|paṭalair dalit'|ândha|kāre
svapn'|ôdyame rahasi saṃmukha|darśan'|ôtthāṃ
lajjā|bhay'|ārta|nayanām anucintayāmi

Ady' âpi tāṃ viraha|vahni|nipīḍit'|âṅgīṃ
tanvīṃ kuraṅga|nayanāṃ surat'|âika|pātram
nānā|vicitra|kṛta|maṇḍanam āvahantīṃ tāṃ
rāja|haṃsa|gamanāṃ su|datīṃ smarāmi

20 Ady' âpi tāṃ vihasitāṃ kuca|bhāra|namrāṃ
muktā|kalāpa|dhavalī|kṛta|kaṇṭha|deśām
tat|keli|mandara|girau kusum'|āyudhasya
kāntāṃ smarāmi rucir'|ôjjvala|puṣpa|ketum

Still when alone I recollect the smile
Which tasted nectar-sweet upon her lip;
I see the fastenings of her braided hair
Slip from their place, and see the garlands slip;
The wandering gaze, the string of pearls which rests
Kissing a pair of full uplifted breasts.

Still I recall how wreaths of jewel lamps,
Garlanded round us in that palace white,
Fragmented darkness with their mass of rays;
Her eyes were pained in modesty and fright
When I surprised her bending over me
To spy her sleeping lover secretly.

Still I remember in her slenderness
The only vessel of my tender pleasure,
Her limbs on fire with separation's flame,
Her teeth as lovely as the various treasure
Of ornaments with which her body shone;
Eyes of a deer, and movements of a swan.

Still I recall my darling as she came,
Bent by her bosom's weight, to pleasure's bower,
House of the god who wounds with fiery darts,
Herself a beautiful and full-blown flower.
Her smile at me was radiance to bedeck
The clustered pearls which gleamed upon her neck.

Ady' âpi cāṭu|śata|durlalit'|ôcit'|ârtham
tasyāḥ smarāmi surata|klama|vihvalāyāḥ
avyakta|nisvanita|kātara|kathyamāna|
saṃkīrṇa|varṇa|ruciraṃ vacanaṃ priyāyāḥ

Ady' âpi tāṃ surata|ghūrṇa|nimīlit'|âkṣīṃ
srast'|âṅga|yaṣṭi|galit'|âṃśuka|keśa|pāśām
śṛṅgāra|vāri|ruha|kānana|rāja|haṃsīṃ
janm'|ântare 'pi nidhane 'py anucintayāmi

Ady' âpi tāṃ praṇayinīṃ mṛga|śāvak'|âkṣīṃ
pīyūṣa|purṇa|kuca|kumbha|yugaṃ vahantīm
paśyāmy ahaṃ yadi punar divas'|âvasāne
svarg'|âpavarga|nara|rāja|sukhaṃ tyajāmi

Ady' âpi tāṃ kṣiti|tale vara|kāminīnāṃ
sarv'|âṅga|sundaratayā pratham'|âika|rekhām
śṛṅgāra|nāṭaka|ras'|ôttama|pāna|pātrīṃ
kāntāṃ smarāmi kusum'|āyudha|bāṇa|khinnām

Still I recall how my beloved spoke
When weary with our play; her tongue, confused,
Wished to assure me of her wild delight
But stumbled on the flatteries she used.
With timid murmurings and accents blurred
How charmingly she jumbled every word.

Still in another life I shall recall
What I recall at this my hour of dying:
The slender body of my royal swan
Amid love's lotus clusters languid lying;
Her eyes were closed in pleasure as we revelled,
Her garment loosened and her hair dishevelled.

Still could I see once more, as day declines
My loving mistress of the fawn-like eyes,
Carrying like two nectar-laden jars
Her swelling breasts, I would for such a prize
Renounce the joys of royalty on earth,
Heavenly bliss, and freedom from rebirth.

Still I recall my darling, whom the shafts
Of love, the flower-arrowed god, distress;
Above the choicest beauties of the earth
She shines with rays of flawless loveliness
As the new moon, the cup from which I savor
Where love is played the play's essential flavor.

25 Ady' âpi tāṃ stimita|vastram iv' âṅga|lagnāṃ
prauḍha|pratāpa|madan'|ânala|tapta|dehām
bālām anātha|śaraṇām anukampanīyāṃ
prāṇ'|âdhikāṃ kṣaṇam ahaṃ na hi vismarāmi

Ady' âpi tāṃ prathamato vara|sundarīṇāṃ
sneh'|âika|pātra|ghaṭitām avan"|īśa|putrīm
tapo janā viraha|jaḥ sukumāra|gātryāḥ
soḍhuṃ na śakyata iti praticintayāmi.

Ady' âpi vismaya|karīṃ tridaśān vihāya
buddhir balāc calati me kim ahaṃ karomi
jānann api pratimuhūrtam ih' ânta|kāle
kānt" êti vallabhatar" êti mam' êti dhīrā.

Ady' âpi tāṃ gamanam ity uditaṃ madīyam
śrutv" âiva bhīru|hariṇīm iva cañcal'|âkṣīm
vācaḥ skhalad|vigalad|aśru|jal'|ākul'|âkṣīṃ
saṃcintayāmi guru|śoka|vinamra|vaktrām

Still I recall her, clinging close to me 25
As a wet garment, while the furious flame
Of passion seared her body, a mere girl
Who more to me than life itself became.
No moment fails the piteous recollection
Of her distress, who lacks her lord's protection.

Still when I think of those of lovely form
My thoughts turn first of all to the princess
Whose tender limbs were surely formed to be
The sole recipients of my tenderness.
My fellow men, this absence from my fair
Burns me with fiercer flame than I can bear.

Still, though I know this is my final hour,
O my bewilderer—what can I do?—
My thoughts are ever and again constrained
To leave the unaging gods and fly to you.
My constant one, I think of you alone
As dearest, as beloved, as my own.

Still I recall her in whose eyes I saw
The shy mobility of a gazelle.
When she had heard that I must go from her
Her tongue would falter on the word "Farewell";
From brimming eyes water of tears would flow,
And with the weight of grief her head hung low.

Ady' âpi jātu nipuṇaṃ yatatā may" âpi
dṛṣṭaṃ dṛśā jagati jāti|vidhe vadhūnām
saundarya|nirjita|rati|dvija|rāja|kānteḥ
kānt"|ānanasya sadṛśām vadanaṃ guṇair na

30 Ady' âpi tāṃ kṣaṇa|viyoga|viṣ'|ôpameyāṃ
saṅge punar bahutarām amṛt'|âbhiṣekām
maj|jīva|dhāraṇa|karīṃ madanāt sa|tandrām
kiṃ Brahma|Keśava|Haraiḥ? su|datīṃ smarāmi

Ady' âpi rāja|gṛhato mayi nīyamane
durvāra|bhīṣaṇa|karair Yama|dūta|kalpaiḥ
kiṃ kiṃ tayā bahuvidhaṃ na kṛtaṃ mad|arthe
vaktuṃ na pāryata iti vyathate mano me

Ady' âpi me niśi divā hṛdayaṃ dunoti
pūrṇ'|êndu|sundara|mukhaṃ mama vallabhāyāḥ
lāvaṇya|nirjita|rati|kṣata|kāma|darpaṃ
bhūyaḥ puraḥ pratipadaṃ na vilokyate yat

Still, though my eye may diligently search
This world, which is so full of every kind
Of comely woman, yet the counterpart
Of my beloved's face I cannot find.
She conquers by the beauty of that face
Both Love's beloved and the moon in grace.

Still I recall the white-toothed girl, from whom
It was poison for a moment to be parted;
Then in renewed embrace anointing me
With copious nectar, she new life imparted,
Herself fatigued by love; if she is mine,
Why do I need the trinity divine?

Still my mind flinches at the memory
How from the royal palace I was led
By fearsome men, who, ineluctable,
Seemed envoys from the ruler of the dead.
In grief I cannot tell how for my sake
There was no effort that she did not make.

Still does it pain my heart by night and day
That I before me may no longer see
At every step I take my darling's face
In full-moon beauty shining upon me.
The god of love is wounded in his pride,
For she is far more charming than his bride.

Ady' âpi tām avihatāṃ manas" âcalena
saṃcintayāmi yuvatīṃ mama jīvit'|āśām
n' âny'|ôpabhukta|nava|yauvana|bhāra|sārāṃ
janm'|ântare 'pi mama s" âiva gatir yathā syāt

Ady' âpi tad|vadana|paṅkaja|gandha|lubdha|
bhrāmyad|dvi|repha|caya|cumbita|gaṇḍa|deśām
līl"|âvadhūta|kara|pallava|kaṅkaṇānāṃ
kvāṇena mūrcchati manaḥ sutarāṃ madīyam

35 Ady' âpi sā nakha|padaṃ stana|maṇḍale yad
dattaṃ may" āsya|madhu|pāna|vimohitena
udbhinna|roma|pulakair bahubhiḥ prayatnāj
jāgarti rakṣati vilokayati smarāmi

Ady' âpi kopa|vimukhī|kṛta|gantu|kāmā
n' ôktaṃ vacaḥ pratidadāti yad" âiva pūrvam
cumbāmi roditi bhṛśaṃ patito 'smi pāde
«dāsas tava priyatame bhaja māṃ» smarāmi

Still I keep all my wavering thoughts on her,
That in my next life she may be my lot,
The essence of whose youth no other man
Has tasted, maiden pure without a spot,
My only hope in this life, and my sum
Of aspirations for the life to come.

Still I recall how when a swam of bees,
Allured by perfume from her lotus face,
Paused in their wanderings to kiss her cheeks,
In self-defence with agitated grace
She waved her bud-like hands, whose bracelets swinging
Distract my mind, for still I hear their ringing.

Still I recall how when I had grown drunk
Upon the wine with which her mouth was filled
Into her rounded breast I pressed my nails
And left a mark at which her body thrilled,
But she would try to watch and be alert,
Seeking to guard herself from further hurt.

Still I remember when in angry mood
She turned her face away and made to go.
I spoke to her, but she would not reply;
I kissed her, and her tears began to flow.
Freely she wept; then at her feet I fell:
"I am your slave my dearest; love me well."

Ady' âpi dhāvati manaḥ kim ahaṃ karomi
sārdhaṃ sakhībhir api vāsa|gṛhe sva|kāntām
kānt"|âṅga|saṃga|parihāsa|vicitra|nṛtye
krīḍ"|âbhirāma iti yātu madīya|kālaḥ

Ady' âpi tāṃ jagati varṇayituṃ na kaś cic
chaknoty adṛṣṭa|sadṛśīṃ ca parigrahaṃ me
dṛṣṭaṃ tayoḥ sadṛśayoḥ khalu yena rūpam
śakto bhaved yadi sa eva paraṃ tu n' ânyaḥ

Ady' âpi tāṃ na khalu vedmi kim īśa|patnī
śāpaṃ gatā sura|pater atha Kṛṣṇa|Lakṣmī
dhātr" âiva kiṃ tri|jagataḥ parimohanāya
sā nirmitā yuvati|ratna|didṛkṣayā vā

40 Ady' âpi te pratimuhuḥ pratibhāvyamānāś
ceto haranti hariṇī|śiśu|locanāyāḥ
antar|nimagna|madhu|p'|ākula|kunda|vṛnda|
sandarbha|sundara|ruco nayan'|ârdha|pātāḥ

Still does my mind run on—what can I do?—
To well-loved rooms in which my darling lay,
Rooms to which lovely women gave their charm
With song and laughter, dance and mime and play.
Where my own love lies with her maiden friends,
There would I pass my time till my time ends.

Still there is no one is the whole wide world
Able to give the picture of my wife,
For on this earth her like has not been seen
Nor shall be seen in this or any life,
And he alone, if even he, could catch
Her likeness, who had seen her beauty's match.

Still I as doubtful: is she Párvati,
Lord Shiva's consort? Shachi, Indra's bride?
Or Lakshmi, Lady Fortune, Krishna's wife?
Did the Creator form her to misguide
The triple world, or with a whim to see
The purest jewel of virginity?

Still when I think, as I have often thought,
To make comparison between the lustre
Of timid glances from her fawn-like eyes
And a wreath woven from a jasmine cluster
Which honey-drinking bees have agitated,
Drowned in the blooms, my mind is captivated.

Ady' âpi nirmala|śarac|chaśi|gaura|kānti
ceto muner api haret kim ut' âsmadīyam
vaktraṃ sudhā|rasa|mayaṃ yadi tat prapadye
cumban pibāmy aviratam vyadhate mano me

Ady' âpi tat|kamala|reṇu|sugandha|gandhi
tat|prema|vāri makara|dhvaja|tāpa|hāri
prāpnomy ahaṃ yadi punaḥ surat'|âika|tīrthaṃ
prāṇāṃs tyajāmi niyataṃ tad|avāpti|hetoḥ

Ady' âpy aho jagati sundara|lakṣa|pūrṇe
any'|ânyam uttama|guṇ'|âdhika|saṃprapanne
anyābhir apy upamituṃ na mayā ca śakyaṃ
rūpaṃ tadīyam iti me hṛdaye viṣadaḥ

Ady' âpi sā mama manas|taṭinīvad āste
romāñca|vīci|vilasat|pulin'|âṅga|yaṣṭiḥ
mat|sv'|ânta|sārasa|calad|virah|ôcca|paṅkāt
kiṃ cid gamaṃ prathayatī priya|rāja|haṃsī

Still now that face of golden loveliness,
A spotless moon upon an autumn night,
That mouth of nectar which absolves from death
Would steal the senses of an anchorite;
So what of me? Could I those lips regain
I'd kiss them and no more feel parting's pain.

Still, could I but attain once more that mouth
Passion's one consecrated bathing-place,
Watered by her affection to assuage
Love's scorching heat, and by her lotus face
Scented with pollen, surely I'd resign
My life in forfeit to preserve it mine.

Still is my heart despondent, for I see
The world alas so crowded to excess
With beauties and their noble qualities;
Yet ever in this myriad loveliness
Not one to serve me for comparison
To her perfection whom I dote upon.

Still now my dear princess, a royal swan
Causing my tender lotus heart to quiver
Stirs from the mud of our separation
As in my mind she flows or like a river;
Her slender body coruscates with thrills,
Like sand-banks glittering beneath the rills.

45 Ady' âpi tāṃ nṛpatī śekhara|rāja|putrīṃ
sampūrṇa|yauvana|madālasa|ghūrṇa|netrīm
gandharva|yakṣa|sura|kiṃnara|nāga|kanyāṃ
sākṣān nabho|nipatitām iva cintayāmi

Ady' âpi tāṃ nija|vapuḥ|kṛśa|vedi|madhyām
uttuṃga|saṃbhṛta|sudhā|stana|kumbha|yugmām
nānā|vicitra|kṛta|maṇḍana|maṇḍit'|âṅgīṃ
supt'|ôtthitāṃ niśi divā na hi vismarāmi

Ady' âpi tāṃ kanaka|kānti|dhṛt'|âlas'|âṅgīṃ
vrīḍ"|ôtsukāṃ madana|bhīti|vikampamānām
aṃg'|âṃga|saṃga|paricumbana|jāta|mohāṃ
maj|jīvan'|âuṣadhim iva pramadāṃ smarāmi

Ady' âpi tat surata|keli|nir|astra|yuddham
bandh'|ôpabandha|patan'|ôtthita|śūnya|hastam
dant'|ōṣṭha|pīḍana|nakha|kṣata|rakta|siktaṃ
tasyāḥ smarāmi rati|bandhura|niṣṭhuratvam

Still I recall that wanton rolling eye
Intoxicated by the prime of youth;
Her father is a very diadem
To crown the kings of men, but she in truth
More like a princess of celestial might
Fallen from heaven to grace our earthly sight.

Still neither night nor day may I forget
My loving mistress as she rose from sleep,
Her varied show of brilliant ornament
Her breasts so close together, tall and steep,
As if above her altar-slender waist
Twin jars of milky nectar had been placed.

Still I recall the physic of my life.
That languid body in its golden charm;
She was uneasy for her modesty
And passion made her tremble with alarm
Till gradually as I pressed limb to limb
My fervent kisses made her senses swim.

Still I recall her sweet tenacity
In pleasure's sport, the battle without arms
In which we varied our embraces as
We rose and fell, and struck with open palms,
Till teeth pressed into lips, and raking nails
Left drops of blood to mark out scarlet trails.

Ady' âpy ahaṃ vara|vadhū|surat'|ôpabhogam
jīvāmi n' ânya|vidhinākṣaṇam antareṇa
tad bhrātaro maraṇam eva hi duḥkha|śāntyai
vijñāpayāmi bhavatas tvaritaṃ lunīdhvam

50 Ady' âpi n' ôjjhati Haraḥ kila kāla|kūṭam
kūrmo bibharti dharaṇīṃ khalu pṛṣṭa|bhāge
ambho|nidhir vahati duḥsaha|vaḍav"|âgnim
aṅgī|kṛtaṃ sukṛtinaḥ paripālayanti

Still in no other fashion can I live,
Nor other profit in this life can find
Than in enjoyment of love's ecstasies
Shared with the dearest of her gentle kind.
Death only, brother, can my pain allay,
So cut me off, I plead, without delay.

Still Vishnu's tortoise back upholds the earth
As when the gods for nectar churned the seas;
Poison and fire then threatened all the world;
One Shiva drank and still will not release,
One Ocean still retains within his deep;
For what the noble have made theirs, they keep.

NOTES

Note references are to verse numbers. 1. = Politics, 2. = Passion, 3. = Disenchantment, 4. = Ámaru, 5. = The Love Thief.

1.5 **Hare's horn:** A famous image in Indian literature, it connotes the futility of looking for something that can never be found.

1.7 **The Arranger:** *(Vidhātā)* is another name for the creator god Brahma in his capacity as distributor of fate and as organizer of the cosmology.

1.15 **Fade away always: (kṣiyante... satatam)** PASSI and STOLER MILLER (following Rāmacandrabudendra) take *satatam* with the following noun, whereas I take it with *kṣiyante* in conformity with the meter and Rāmarṣi's commentary.

1.18 Stoler Miller p.55 translates the qualities as residing in the individual categories of people. This is possible but stretches the grammar and goes against the commentators and other translators.

1.26 **Rahu**, lord of the Dánavas, is a celestial demon who is the cause of eclipses.

1.28 Originally mountains had wings. Indra cut them off with his thunderbolts, but Himálaya's son, the mountain Maínaka, escaped by plunging into the sea, an act of cowardice which pained his father.

1.40 **Meru** is the mountain which stands at the centre of the earth; its summit touches the lowest heaven.

1.42 In Indian literary convention, the cobra's head contains a **jewel**.

1.49 The reference is to the shadow of the sun, as on a sundial, which disappears at noon.

1.56 I.e. like walking on a razor's edge.

1.66 As the milk begins to boil, first water is put on the fire, but then it starts to overboil and is cooled by adding water.

1.68 **Brahma's egg** is the Hindu cosmos; it rests on a tortoise and its highest point is Dhruva, the Pole Star.

1.91b [included as a second 91].

1.96 Possessing valuable means, people misuse them for paltry ends. **Camphor** fragments are an insecticide, ***kodrava*** the poorest kind of edible grain. Birth as a human being is one's only chance to aquire good karman, e.g. by austerities, but people waste it.

2.21 On the meaning of this poem see PASSI, *op.cit.* n.1 p.121.

3.40 This pronoun designates the neuter Brahman, the highest object of meditation and spiritual attainment.

3.61 **Wish-granting gems**: a jewel capable of granting every desire.

3.69 ***Yasya*** **with That**. See note ad §1.1 above.

5.13 See Introduction: this translation covers both the Sanskrit verse opposite and another (v. 12 in the edition mainly read), which runs:

Ady' âpi tat/kanaka/kuṇḍala/ghṛṣṭa/gaṇḍam
āsyaṃ smarāmi viparīta/rat'/âbhiyoge
āndolana/śrama/jala/sphuṭa/sāndra/bindu
muktā/phala/prakara/vicchuritaṃ priyāyāḥ.

INDEX

INDEX

Sanskrit words are given according to the accented CSL pronuncuation aid in the English alphabetical order. They are followed by the conventional diacritics in brackets.

THE CLAY SANSKRIT LIBRARY

The volumes in the series are listed here in order of publication.
Titles marked with an asterisk* are also available in the
Digital Clay Sanskrit Library (eCSL).
For further information visit www.claysanskritlibrary.org

1. The Emperor of the Sorcerers (*Bṛhatkathāślokasaṃgraha*) (vol. 1 of 2) by *Budhasvāmin*. Sir James Mallinson
2. Heavenly Exploits (*Divyāvadāna*). Joel Tatelman
3. Maha·bhárata III: The Forest (*Vanaparvan*) (vol. 4 of 4)* William J. Johnson
4. Much Ado about Religion (*Āgamaḍambara*) by *Bhaṭṭa Jayanta*. Csaba Dezső
5. The Birth of Kumára (*Kumārasaṃbhava*) by *Kālidāsa*. David Smith
6. Ramáyana I: Boyhood (*Bālakāṇḍa*) by *Vālmīki*. Robert P. Goldman
7. The Epitome of Queen Lilávati (*Līlāvatīsāra*) (vol. 1 of 2) by *Jinaratna*. R.C.C. Fynes
8. Ramáyana II: Ayódhya (*Ayodhyākāṇḍa*) by *Vālmīki*. Sheldon I. Pollock
9. Love Lyrics (*Amaruśataka, Śatakatraya & Caurapañcāśikā*) by *Amaru, Bhartṛhari & Bilhaṇa*. Greg Bailey & Richard Gombrich
10. What Ten Young Men Did (*Daśakumāracarita*) by *Daṇḍin*. Isabelle Onians
11. Three Satires (*Kaliviḍambana, Kalāvilāsa & Bhallaṭaśataka*) by *Nīlakaṇṭha, Kṣemendra & Bhallaṭa*. Somadeva Vasudeva
12. Ramáyana IV: Kishkíndha (*Kiṣkindhākāṇḍa*) by *Vālmīki*. Rosalind Lefeber
13. The Emperor of the Sorcerers (*Bṛhatkathāślokasaṃgraha*) (vol. 2 of 2) by *Budhasvāmin*. Sir James Mallinson
14. Maha·bhárata IX: Shalya (*Śalyaparvan*) (vol. 1 of 2)* Justin Meiland

15. Rákshasa's Ring (*Mudrārākṣasa*)*
by *Viśākhadatta*. Michael Coulson
16. Messenger Poems (*Meghadūta, Pavanadūta & Haṃsadūta*)
by *Kālidāsa, Dhoyī & Rūpa Gosvāmin*. Sir James Mallinson
17. Ramáyana III: The Forest (*Araṇyakāṇḍa*)
by *Vālmīki*. Sheldon I. Pollock
18. The Epitome of Queen Lilávati (*Līlāvatīsāra*) (vol. 2 of 2)
by *Jinaratna*. R.C.C. Fynes
19. Five Discourses on Worldly Wisdom (*Pañcatantra*)*
by *Viṣṇuśarman*. Patrick Olivelle
20. Ramáyana V: Súndara (*Sundarakāṇḍa*) by *Vālmīki*.
Robert P. Goldman & Sally J. Sutherland Goldman
21. Maha·bhárata II: The Great Hall (*Sabhāparvan*)
Paul Wilmot
22. The Recognition of Shakúntala (*Abhijñānaśākuntala*) (Kashmir Recension) by *Kālidāsa*. Somadeva Vasudeva
23. Maha·bhárata VII: Drona (*Droṇaparvan*) (vol. 1 of 4)*
Vaughan Pilikian
24. Rama Beyond Price (*Anargharāghava*)
by *Murāri*. Judit Törzsök
25. Maha·bhárata IV: Viráta (*Virāṭaparvan*)
Kathleen Garbutt
26. Maha·bhárata VIII: Karna (*Karṇaparvan*) (vol. 1 of 2)
Adam Bowles
27. "The Lady of the Jewel Necklace" & "The Lady who Shows her Love" (*Ratnāvalī & Priyadarśikā*) by *Harṣa*.*
Wendy Doniger
28. The Ocean of the Rivers of Story (*Kathāsaritsāgara*) (vol. 1 of 7)
by *Somadeva*. Sir James Mallinson
29. Handsome Nanda (*Saundarananda*)*
by *Aśvaghoṣa*. Linda Covill
30. Maha·bhárata IX: Shalya (*Śalyaparvan*) (vol. 2 of 2)*
Justin Meiland
31. Rama's Last Act (*Uttararāmacarita*) by *Bhavabhūti*.
Sheldon Pollock. Foreword by Girish Karnad

32. “Friendly Advice” (*Hitopadeśa*) by *Nārāyaṇa* &
 “King Víkrama’s Adventures” (*Vikramacarita*). Judit Törzsök
33. Life of the Buddha (*Buddhacarita*)
 by *Aśvaghoṣa*. Patrick Olivelle
34. Maha·bhárata V: Preparations for War (*Udyogaparvan*) (vol. 1 of 2)
 Kathleen Garbutt. Foreword by Gurcharan Das
35. Maha·bhárata VIII: Karna (*Karṇaparvan*) (vol. 2 of 2)
 Adam Bowles
36. Maha·bhárata V: Preparations for War (*Udyogaparvan*) (vol. 2 of 2)
 Kathleen Garbutt
37. Maha·bhárata VI: Bhishma (*Bhīṣmaparvan*) (vol. 1 of 2)*
 Including the “Bhagavad Gita” in Context
 Alex Cherniak. Foreword by Ranajit Guha
38. The Ocean of the Rivers of Story (*Kathāsaritsāgara*) (vol. 2 of 7)
 by *Somadeva*. Sir James Mallinson
39. “How the Nagas were Pleased” (*Nāgānanda*) by *Harṣa* &
 “The Shattered Thighs” (*Ūrubhaṅga*) by *Bhāsa*.*
 Andrew Skilton
40. Gita·govínda: Love Songs of Radha and Krishna (*Gītagovinda*)*
 by *Jayadeva*. Lee Siegel. Foreword by Sudipta Kaviraj
41. “Bouquet of Rasa” & “River of Rasa” (*Rasamañjarī & Rasataraṅ-giṇī*) by *Bhānudatta*. Sheldon Pollock
42. Garland of the Buddha’s Past Lives (*Jātakamālā*) (vol. 1 of 2)*
 by *Āryaśūra*. Justin Meiland
43. Maha·bhárata XII: Peace (*Śāntiparvan*) (vol. 3 of 5)*
 “The Book of Liberation” (*Mokṣadharma*). Alexander Wynne
44. The Little Clay Cart (*Mṛcchakaṭikā*) by *Śūdraka*.
 Diwakar Acharya. Foreword by Partha Chatterjee
45. Bhatti’s Poem: The Death of Rávana (*Bhaṭṭikāvya*)*
 by *Bhaṭṭi*. Oliver Fallon

46. "Self-Surrender," "Peace," "Compassion," and "The Mission of the Goose": Poems and Prayers from South India (*Ātmārpaṇastuti, Śāntivilāsa, Dayāśataka & Haṃsasaṃdeśa*) by *Appayya Dīkṣita, Nīlakaṇṭha Dīkṣita & Vedānta Deśika.* Yigal Bronner & David Shulman
Foreword by Gieve Patel
47. Maha·bhárata VI: Bhishma (*Bhīṣmaparvan*) (vol. 2 of 2)* Alex Cherniak
48. How Úrvashi Was Won (*Vikramorvaśīya*) by *Kālidāsa* Velcheru Narayana Rao & David Shulman
49. The Quartet of Causeries (*Caturbhāṇī*) by *Śūdraka, Śyāmilaka, Vararuci & Īśvaradatta.* Csaba Dezső & Somadeva Vasudeva
50. Garland of the Buddha's Past Lives (*Jātakamālā*) (vol. 2 of 2)* by *Āryaśūra.* Justin Meiland
51. Princess Kadámbari (*Kādambarī*) (vol. 1 of 3) by *Bāṇa.* David Smith
52. The Rise of Wisdom Moon (*Prabodhacandrodaya*)* by *Kṛṣṇamiśra.* Matthew T. Kapstein
Foreword by J.N. Mohanty
53. Maha·bhárata VII: Drona (*Droṇaparvan*) (vol. 2 of 4)* Vaughan Pilikian
54. Maha·bhárata X & XI: Dead of Night & The Women (*Sauptikaparvan & Strīparvan*).* Kate Crosby
55. Seven Hundred Elegant Verses (*Āryāsaptaśatī*)* by *Govardhana.* Friedhelm Hardy
56. Málavika and Agni·mitra (*Mālavikāgnimitram*) by *Kālidāsa.* Dániel Balogh & Eszter Somogyi

Permitted finals:

k	ṭ	t	p	ṅ	n	m	*(Except āḥ/aḥ)* ḥ/r	āḥ	aḥ	*Initial letters:*
k	ṭ	t	p	ṅ	n	ṃ	ḥ	āḥ	aḥ	k/kh
g	ḍ	d	b	ṅ	n	ṃ	r	ā	o	g/gh
k	ṭ	c	p	ṅ	ṃś	ṃ	ś	āś	aś	c/ch
g	ḍ	j	b	ṅ	ñ	ṃ	r	ā	o	j/jh
k	ṭ	ṭ	p	ṅ	ṃṣ	ṃ	ṣ	āṣ	aṣ	ṭ/ṭh
g	ḍ	ḍ	b	ṅ	ṇ	ṃ	r	ā	o	ḍ/ḍh
k	ṭ	t	p	ṅ	ṃs	ṃ	s	ās	as	t/th
g	ḍ	d	b	ṅ	n	ṃ	r	ā	o	d/dh
k	ṭ	t	p	ṅ	n	ṃ	ḥ	āḥ	aḥ	p/ph
g	ḍ	d	b	ṅ	n	ṃ	r	ā	o	b/bh
ṅ	ṇ	n	m	ṅ	n	ṃ	r	ā	o	*nasals* (n/m)
g	ḍ	d	b	ṅ	n	ṃ	r	ā	o	y/v
g	ḍ	d	b	ṅ	n	ṃ	*zero*[1]	ā	o	r
g	ḍ	l	b	ṅ	l̃[2]	ṃ	r	ā	o	l
k	ṭ	c ch	p	ṅ	ñ ś/ch	ṃ	ḥ	āḥ	aḥ	ś
k	ṭ	t	p	ṅ	n	ṃ	ḥ	āḥ	aḥ	ṣ/s
gg h	ḍḍ h	dd h	bb h	ṅ	n	ṃ	r	ā	o	h
g	ḍ	d	b	ṅ/ṅṅ[3]	n/nn[3]	m	r	ā	a[4]	*vowels*
k	ṭ	t	p	ṅ	n	m	ḥ	āḥ	aḥ	*zero*

[1]ḥ or r disappears, and if a/i/u precedes, this lengthens to ā/ī/ū. [2]e.g. tān+lokān=tāl̃ lokān. [3]The doubling occurs if the preceding vowel is short. [4]Except: aḥ+a=o '.